knitted
BASKETS

42 Hip, Happy, and Handmade Projects
to Keep Your World Organized

Nola Heidbreder & Linda Pietz

SPRING HOUSE PRESS

DEDICATION
Soli Deo Gloria

THANKS
Many thanks to the dedicated knitters who helped us by knitting the beautiful baskets!
Bradley Duck: Ozark Basket
Priscilla Pietz: Nesting Modular Baskets
Heidi Rietjens: Fluffy the Basket
Leslie Rogers: Bad Hair Day, Button Beauty
Megan Senini: All Zipped Up, Berry Basket, Folk Art Basket

knitted
BASKETS

Front cover: Field of Poppies, page 92.
Back cover: Nesting Modular Baskets, page 108.

Publisher: Paul McGahren
Editorial Director: Matthew Teague
Editor: Kerri Grzybicki
Design: Lindsay Hess
Layout: Jodie Delohery
Illustration: Carolyn Mosher
Photography: Danielle Atkins
Technical Editor: Tian Connaughton

Spring House Press
P.O. Box 239
Whites Creek, TN 37189
ISBN: 978-1-940611-60-0

Library of Congress Control Number: 2017963739
Printed in the United States of America
First Printing: March 2018

Note: The following list contains names used in *Knitted Baskets* that may be registered with the United States Copyright Office: Berroco (Vintage); B.F. Goodrich Company; *Braveheart; Brigadoon;* Brown Sheep Company, Inc. (Lamb's Pride, Wildfoote Luxury Sock yarn); Cascade (220); Clover (Hana-Ami Flower Loom, Mini Flower Loom); Craft Yarn Council; Denise; Dewberry Ridge (Star Li'l Weaver Pin Loom); DMC (Pearl Cotton Variations); Embellish-Knit!; Georges Seurat; Gideon Sundback; *Hamish Macbeth;* James Cagney; Kool-Aid; Lacis; Life Savers; Lion Brand Yarns (Fisherman's Wool); Louis Comfort Tiffany; *Outlander;* Pattiewack; Red Heart (Super Saver); *Rob Roy;* The Morse Museum; *Yankee Doodle Dandy;* Yummy Yarns (Jelly Yarn); Wool Novelty Company.

To learn more about Spring House Press books, or to find a retailer near you, email info@springhousepress.com or visit us at www.springhousepress.com.

From back to front: Exotic, page 86; Faux Basketweave Basket, page 33; Seurat Reimagined, page 112.

contents

getting started with knitting

Whether you are a pro at knitting or completely new to the hobby, this section provides the basic information and techniques you need to know to succeed.

Knitting is the process of adding a small yarn segment to a yarn loop on a needle to prevent unraveling. Each loop on the needle is called a **stitch,** and a series of stitches is called a row. To knit a row, a series of stitches is on a holding needle in one hand while the other hand holds the working needle that is making the next row of stitches. The working needle point is inserted into 1 stitch at a time on the tip of the holding needle; the point of the working needle then brings a short length of yarn up through the stitch onto the working needle, forming a new stitch that stays on the working needle, while the previous stitch is removed from the holding needle. As each stitch is knit, the row gradually transfers from one needle to the other. When the last stitch has been knit, the row is finished and the work is turned, and the knitter exchanges the full needle and the empty needle in her or his hands and is ready to knit the next row.

Before knitting a row, the first set of stitches needs to be mounted onto one of the knitting needles to form a foundation or base row. This is called casting on stitches. After the base row is created, you'll continue by knitting and purling stitches as called for to create different textures. You'll also need to increase and decrease stitches to modify the size of the finished fabric. The final step is to bind or cast off to keep your project from unraveling.

Note that illustrations show the process for right-handed knitters. Left-handed knitters should follow the instructions, substituting RH (right-hand) for LH (left-hand) and LH for RH. You could also scan or photograph the illustrations and

flip them with your camera or computer software to see the stitches from a left-handed knitter's perspective.

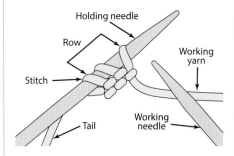

ABOUT KNITTING NEEDLES

Knitting needles become your close companions and are, after all, the main tools of the trade, but each knitter will uncover a few favorites after years of trial and error. There are 3 main features of needles that determine which will become your go-to sets:

- Material they are made of and their finish

- Points

- Length

In the case of circular needles, which are used to knit in the round:

- The join where the cable meets the needles

- The cable itself

Needles are made of plastic, acrylic, fiberglass, different woods, and metal. Depending on the needle manufacturer, these are then coated with resin, varnish, laminate, or chrome. The points of the

needle can be blunt or extremely sharp. The length of the point from tip to where it reaches the actual circumference of the needle varies from brand to brand, or sometimes within one company's range of needles. Double-pointed needles, which come in sets of 4 or 5, are used for knitting small cylinders in the round. Circular needles have a cable between 2 needle tips that are interchangeable and are used for larger cylindrical knitting. However, some cables are deliberately more flexible, which allows for in-the-round techniques like the "magic loop" method.

There have been 3 common needle size numbering systems in English-speaking countries for the last century: UK and Commonwealth sizes, U.S. sizes, and metric sizes in millimeters. There is still inconsistency between manufacturers with U.S. sizes. The UK sizes are no longer used, but if you are given old needles, you may find some with this counter-intuitive numbering system where the larger the number on the needle, the smaller its circumference. The metric system is universal and more accurate, and is becoming the standard. See the U.S. versus metric knitting needle sizes chart on page 122.

Many well-meaning grandmotherly types recommend learning to knit with acrylic yarn and plastic needles, mainly because you will invest less in start-up materials this way, just in case you don't take to knitting. Unfortunately, this frustrates beginners to no end. Acrylic yarn is plastic, and when you rub plastic yarn against plastic needles you get friction, heat, resistance, and a squeaky sound. As a beginner, you're more likely to knit too tightly because you are afraid of dropping stitches, and tight knitting plus plastic is a recipe for disaster. Plastic needles also tend to be blunt, which makes it hard to insert the needle into tight spaces. Using a wood or bamboo needle set that has a light varnish on it (not too glossy) is a good place to begin. Later, when you are working with very slippery yarns like mohair or alpaca, you may want some acrylic or plastic needles so that your stitches don't simply fly off your needles when you need them to stay put a little. Metal needles are the favorite of many knitters because yarn glides well on them and they don't break.

KNITTING STYLES

There are many ways to hold the needles and yarn and you will develop your own way that suits your finger strength and coordination. When you knit, it's also important to maintain a little tension on the working yarn so that your knitting isn't too loose. It's also key to not overtighten your yarn as you work. Whether you are a right-handed or left-handed knitter, there are 2 ways to feed yarn to your needles to create stitches: English and Continental. There are pros and cons to each style, but try both and see which one suits you best. Whether you knit English or Continental style, whichever you learn first and practice the most will be the easiest down the road, and the other style will feel like riding a unicycle after being used to a bicycle. Within each of the 2 approaches, there are still many variations; these have been passed along over the generations and, in some cases, have become entrenched in geographic areas, earning them names from those areas, such as Scottish, Irish, or Portuguese knitting. The best is to learn both approaches, so that when you want to work 2 colors at the same time, you can knit one color with English style and one color with Continental style.

English-Style Knitting

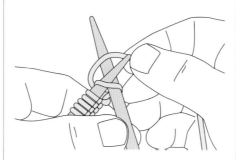

If you wrap the yarn with the dominant hand around the needle held in your dominant hand, you will be "throwing" your stitches. This is also known as English-style knitting. The benefits to English knitting are that most written patterns and shaping techniques, such as decreases, were devised by English knitters, so the way the stitches look on the needles and the angles of insertion will match. The weaknesses of the English style include more arm, hand, and finger movements than in Continental, which accounts for the common perception that English knitting is slower. However, there are English-style knitters who can outpace Continental knitters, so the stereotype is not 100% accurate.

Continental-Style Knitting

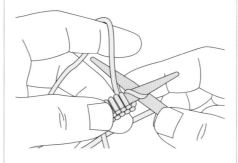

If you have the yarn coming over either the index or middle finger of your non-dominant hand and you scoop the yarn through the stitch with your dominant-hand needle, you will be "picking" your stitches. This is also known as Continental-style knitting. The benefits to Continental knitting are that you use fewer movements, and for many,

this means faster knitting. The main weakness with Continental knitting regards the purl stitch. There are 3 different ways to purl in the Continental technique. The German purl involves one of the fingers of the left hand, usually the index finger, having to work an extra flick motion to get the yarn around the needle. The Norwegian purl keeps the yarn at the back of the work, but includes some extra-fancy maneuvering, which, once you master it, makes you look like a magician. The Eastern purl is fast, but it leaves the stitches oriented incorrectly on the needle for subsequent rows, and one must knit in the back loop of the next row to reorient the stitch. This makes certain decreases and cable stitches on the knit-side rows slower to master because stitches must be slipped to the right-hand needle and back again to untwist them before proceeding to decrease or cross stitches over each other.

KNITTED CAST ON

1 Begin by making a slipknot. Cross the tail (the short end) of the yarn under the yarn that goes to the ball (the working yarn) to form a ring.

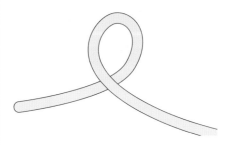

2 Place ring on top of working end of yarn.

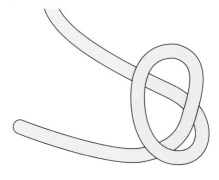

3 Insert the tip of one knitting needle over the crossed yarns, under the strand of working yarn that is below, and then over the top of the ring.

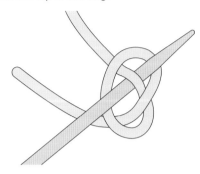

4 Pull on the tail. The slipknot is complete.

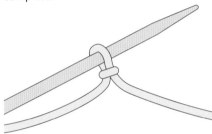

5 Insert 2nd (RH) needle into the loop that is on the first (LH) needle so that it also goes under the LH needle.

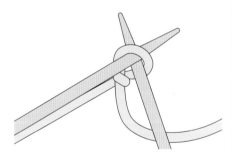

6 Bring the working yarn around the needle from back to front, under and then up and over the RH needle.

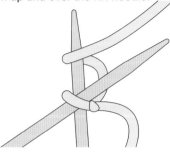

7 Wrap the yarn enough so you can see a small segment of the working yarn under the LH needle (the highlighted section).

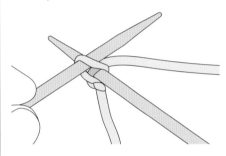

8 With the tip of the RH needle, carefully lift the segment of working yarn and bring it forward through the loop on the LH needle, ending with the RH needle across the top of the LH needle.

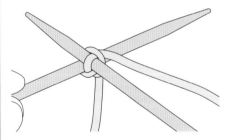

9 Rotate the RH needle so it is almost parallel to the LH needle.

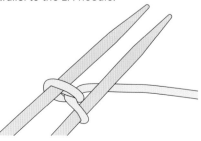

10 Slide the tip of the LH needle toward the loops just enough so you can insert it under the loop on the RH needle.

11 Slide the RH needle out of the loop and tighten the loop gently (never too tightly) on the LH needle.

12 Repeat steps 5–11 until you have the desired number of stitches on the LH needle.

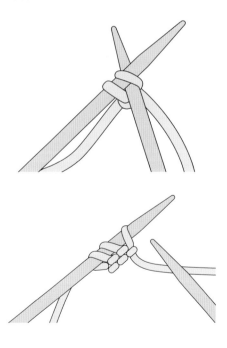

STITCH ORIENTATION

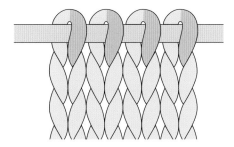

Once you have cast on the necessary number of stitches, it will be time to knit across the first row. A very important skill in knitting is reading your stitches. This means seeing the different ways the yarn or yarn loops are positioned so that you can get the results you want. Look at the stitches that are resting on your LH needle. Notice that the stitches have a "leg" of yarn that is in front of the needle and another "leg" that is in the back of the needle. The right leg should be closer to the tip of the needle and the left leg should be closer to the back end of the needle. In the illustration, the front legs are shaded. This is the standard position of a stitch on the needle. If your stitches don't sit like this, you are wrapping the yarn the wrong way around the needles when you are making new stitches, which twists them in the opposite direction.

THE STITCHES

There are only 2 stitches in knitting: the knit stitch and the purl (pronounced pearl) stitch. The way the knit and purl stitches are worked can be altered slightly to achieve a different look, and it's the combination of the 2 stitches that create texture and stitch patterns.

Knit Stitch (k)

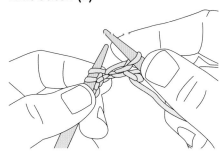

To work a knit stitch, the yarn has to be "to the back" of the work. You've already learned the first half of the knit stitch. Work steps 5–8 of the knitted cast on. From that step, continue as follows:

Use your RH index finger to keep the new loop on the RH needle and to push the old loop off the LH needle. At the same time, use your LH index finger to keep the next loops safely on the LH needle.

Repeat the steps, making sure to add a new loop into the next one on the LH needle and then keep the new loop on the RH needle while slipping a loop off the LH needle. When you have knit all the stitches on the LH needle, you have knit your first row. Flip your RH needle over so that it goes into your left hand and the tip is pointing to the right. You are now ready to start your next row.

Purl Stitch (p)

To work a purl stitch, the yarn has to be "to the front" of the work. This means that you bring the yarn forward between the needle tips so it is on the front of the fabric.

1 Insert the RH needle tip under the front leg of the next stitch on the left needle from below. Move the tip from the right to the left; catch the front leg of the next stitch and bring the needle tip so it is across the top of the LH needle.

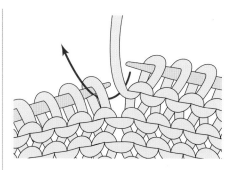

2 Wrap the yarn counterclockwise around the RH needle tip.

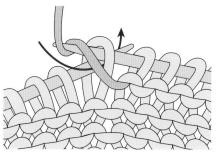

3 With the RH needle tip, move the yarn back through the stitch on the LH needle, keeping it on the RH needle.

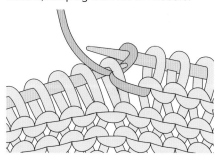

4 Slip the stitch off the LH needle, then tighten the loop on the RH needle so that it's roughly the same size as the other stitches on the needles. Repeat steps 1–4 across to purl the whole row.

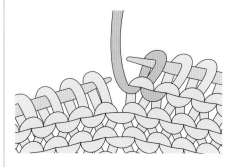

Slip Stitch (sl)

To work a slip stitch, you simply move a loop from the LH needle over to the RH needle by transferring it without wrapping and lifting any yarn. Leave the yarn at the back of the work unless you are told otherwise.

Slip knitwise by inserting the RH needle tip into the front leg as if you were going to knit it, being sure the yarn stays to the back of the work.

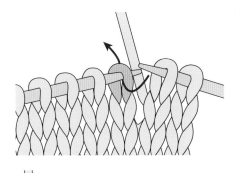

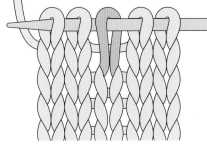

Slip purlwise by inserting the RH needle tip into the front leg of the stitch from the back as if you were going to purl it. Again, the yarn should stay at the back of the work. Slipping purlwise is the standard way to slip a stitch so that its orientation is correct for following rows. If it's not stated explicitly, slip purlwise to be safe.

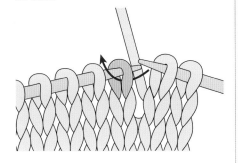

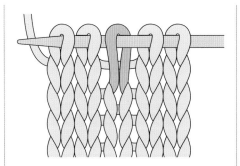

STITCH PATTERNS

The combinations of knit stitches and rows and purl stitches and rows create unique textures. Some of these are used very frequently in knitted fabric and have their own names.

Stockinette Stitch

This stitch pattern looks like a series of Vs or hearts that are side by side and stacked on top of each other. To knit stockinette stitch, you repeat one row of knit stitches followed by one row of purl stitches. These 2 rows make the pattern. In many knitting designs, the knit-row side is considered the public or right side of the fabric.

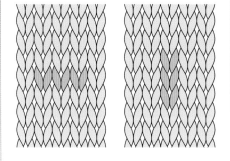

Reverse Stockinette Stitch

This stitch pattern is the reverse side of the stockinette stitch pattern; it looks like rows of bumps that face up and down and are a half-stitch off from each other. In many knitting designs the reverse stockinette side of the fabric is considered the wrong side of the fabric.

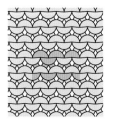 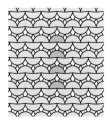

Slip 1 with Yarn in Front (sl1 wyif)

1 Bring yarn forward between the needles.

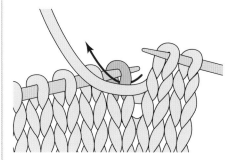

2 Insert the RH needle into the first stitch as if to purl and slip it off the LH needle.

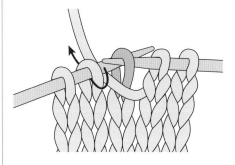

3 Return the yarn to the back side of the

work between the needles. Remaining stitches are knit as usual.

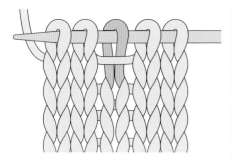

Slip 1 with Yarn in Back (sl1 wyib)

Retain or move yarn to the back of the work between the needles; insert the RH needle into the first stitch as if to purl and slip it off the LH needle.

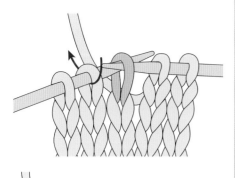

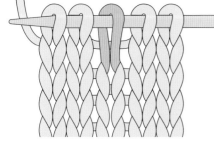

Garter Stitch

This stitch pattern looks similar to purl rows, but the ridges of bumps are separated by small gullies. To work garter stitch, you simply knit every row. Purling every row has the same effect.

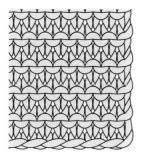

Right vs Wrong Side (RS/WS)

The right side of the knitting doesn't mean that the wrong side is inferior; it simply means that the right side is the public side. Every other row you will be knitting on the right side of the project. Instructions will usually say which side of the fabric will be the right side.

INCREASING STITCHES

Unlike sewing, where the fabric can be cut into different shapes, knit fabric must be given its shape as you create it, so it's necessary to increase the number of stitches you need or to decrease the total used in a given row.

Make One (M1)

1 This is the most invisible way to increase. Look for the horizontal strand of yarn between 2 stitches when you separate the 2 needles slightly. Insert the LH needle from behind under the strand.

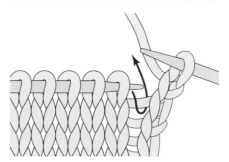

2 Insert the tip of the RH needle under the front strand and below the LH needle.

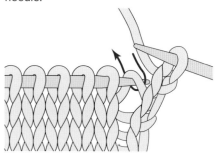

3 Knit the stitch as usual, resulting in a newly formed twisted stitch.

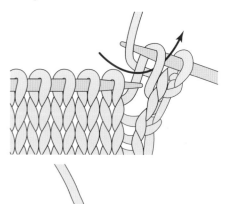

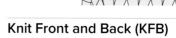

Knit Front and Back (KFB)

Insert RH needle into front leg of first stitch on LH needle. Wrap RH needle and draw yarn through the loop on the LH needle; without removing the stitch from the LH needle, rotate the RH needle and knit into the back leg of the same stitch. Slides stitch off the LH needle.

Yarn-Over Increase, Purl Side

1 To work a yarn-over increase on a purl side, wrap the yarn around the RH needle once; then continue to purl across.

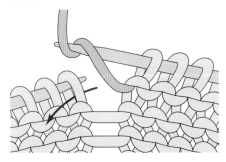

2 On following rows, knit or purl into the yarn-over strand to create a new column of stitches.

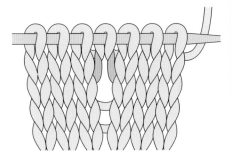

Yarn-Over Increase, Knit Side

1 A yarn-over increase creates an eyelet, which is often used as a design detail. To work a yarn-over increase on a knit side, bring the yarn forward to the front of the work, then knit the next stitch.

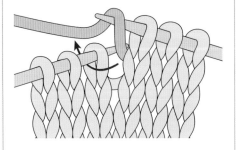

2 This will create an extra diagonal strand that will become a stitch.

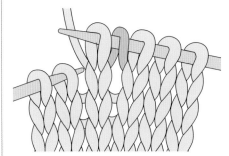

DECREASING STITCHES

When you decrease, diagonal lines are created that are visible in the fabric. It's necessary to decrease 2 different ways so that you have tidy diagonal lines that lean either way, which makes the knit fabric look symmetrical.

Knit 2 Together (k2tog)

1 Insert the tip of the RH needle first under the 2nd stitch on the LH needle and immediately under the front leg of the first stitch on the LH needle.

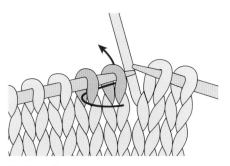

2 Wrap the yarn as usual.

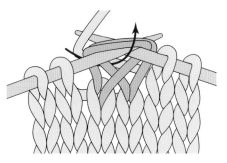

3 Knit the 2 stitches together. This creates a right-leaning diagonal.

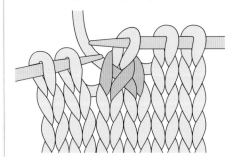

Pass Slipped Stitch Over (PSSO)

With LH needle, lift front loop of 2nd stitch on RH needle and pass entire stitch over first loop on RH needle; drop stitch from needle.

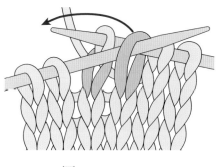

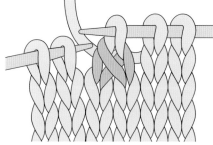

Slip Slip Knit (ssk)

1 With yarn at the back, insert the tip of the RH needle as if to knit the next stitch and slip it without knitting it. Insert the tip of the RH needle as if to purl the next stitch and slip it without purling it.

2 Insert the tip of the LH needle back into both slipped stitches on the RH needle and transfer them back together.

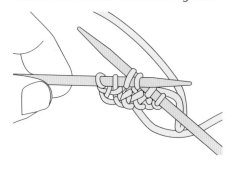

3 Insert the tip of the RH through both back legs of the 2 stitches on the LH and knit them together. This creates a left-leaning diagonal.

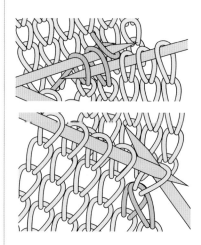

BINDING OFF

When you are done knitting and you don't want your fabric to unravel and come apart, you need to keep the stitches secure. This is called binding or casting off. There are many ways to bind off, but the 2 easiest ways create a nice chainlike edge at the top of the work.

Right-Side Bind Off

If you are about to work a right-side row, knit 2 stitches together through their back legs. Return the stitch you just made to the LH needle. Repeat.

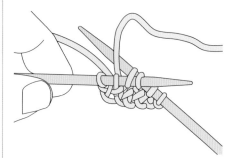

Wrong-Side Bind Off

If you are about to work a wrong-side row, purl 2 stitches together through their front legs. Return the stitch you just made to the LH needle. Repeat.

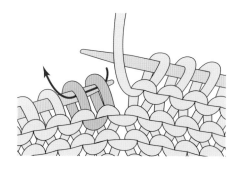

I-Cord Bind Off

This technique is also called applied I-cord. A narrow tube of stockinette stitches is worked across an edge of live knit stitches to both bind-off and create a decorative edge.

1 With the right-side of the work facing, and all stitches on the LH needle, knit cast-on 4 stitches. *Knit 3, ssk with next 2 stitches, return the 4 stitches to the LH needle. Repeat from * once. There are about 4 rounds of I-cord to every 3 stitches on the needle, so the next repeat is worked as follows: Knit 3, slip 3 next stitches as if to purl, return all three to the LH needle as a group, and knit the 3 together through the back loops.

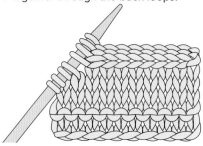

2 Then go back to the * and repeat all the way across the row. Bind off the I-cord stitches when there are only 4 stitches on the LH needle.

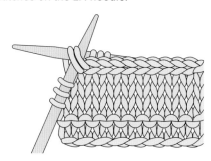

Nesting Modular Baskets, page 108.

FINISHING

Wet Felting

First, either by hand or in a top-loading washing machine, immerse your 100% animal-fiber knit project into warm or hot water with soap or detergent for delicate fabrics. The hand-knit projects are usually made at a looser than normal gauge for the given yarn. Agitate for a period of time and be sure to track this amount of time so you can replicate the process later. The agitation causes the individual fibers in the yarn to interlock with each other, which is a way to deliberately shrink the hand-knit item into a smaller item. The knit stitches will become invisible and fuse together into felt. You may need to immerse and agitate several times until you achieve the designed effect. Squeeze out the excess water and lay into the shape you desire when dry.

Needle Felting

Second, using an individual or a set of felting needles (sharp, barbed needles that look like sewing machine needles without eyes), poke into a small handheld bundle of unspun fibers (usually sheep's wool) over a foundation block of sponge. The barbs on the hook pull the lower fibers up through the upper ones and create a locked-in network of fibers that eventually, with enough hooking, becomes impossible to undo. This is used to felt 3-D objects.

Duplicate Stitch

This technique involves using a tapestry needle and a contrasting color of yarn to work surface stitches that mimic stockinette stitches. This is used to add small sections of color onto a plain background. It is important to make the signature V shape of a knit stitch.

1 Bring up the tapestry needle tip at the base of a V.

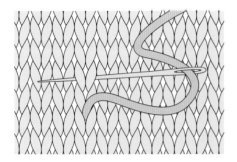

2 Insert the needle under both strands of the V in the stitch above it. Return the needle through the same point as the beginning insertion point at the base of the V and into the base of the next V you want to cover.

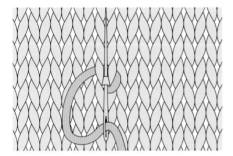

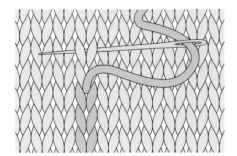

I-Cord

This knitting technique is the abbreviation of Elizabeth Zimmerman's name for the "idiot cord" that is used to keep two mittens attached so they don't get separated from each other. With a pair of double-pointed needles, cast on 3 or 4 stitches. *Knit across and slide the stitches to the other end of the needle, then knit across again, tugging the yarn after knitting the first stitch to draw the far edge closer to the right edge. Repeat from * until the cord is the desired length. A French loom or a spool loom is another way to make I-cord.

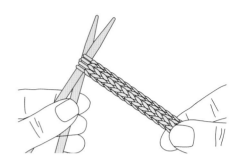

Cookie Cutter Christmas Basket, page 21; the trees are duplicate stitched.

ozark basket

4 MEDIUM

FINISHED MEASUREMENTS: 3-in. wide by 1-in. high
GAUGE: Not applicable due to felting

The Ozarks are a magical and mysterious region of the country. Growing up, we spent a great deal of time there swimming, fishing, and floating. Underneath the surface is a labyrinth of caves filled with dripping stalactites meeting their counterpart stalagmites. Clear rushing springs gush forth water from underneath the earth as the head waters of untold rivers and streams. The brave and hearty people of the region have farmed in vain, for the soil is rocky. The only things that grow well there are trees. This basket is a tribute to the unmatched beauty of the area.

MATERIALS & TOOLS

- 1 skein each Cascade 220 yarn (3½ oz/220 yds), in the following colors:
  - 2429 Irelande (color A)
  - 2445 Shire (color B)
- U.S. size 10 double-pointed needles
- Big eye beading needle
- Sewing needle
- Tube of size 11 seed beads, mixed green, yellow, and brown
- Matching quilting thread
- Stitch markers

NOTE: Gauge is not applicable to this basket. The knitting will be loose to felt better.

SIDES

Using color A, CO 48 sts, distributing them evenly over 3 needles. Join into round, making sure not to twist sts.

Rnd 1: Purl.

Rnd 2: Knit.

Rnd 3: Purl. Break yarn and join color B.

Rnd 4: Knit.

Rnd 5: Slip the first st pwise, k to the end. This will keep basket from having that color change jog.

Rnd 6: Knit.

K every rnd rnd until knitting measures 3 inches from the beginning.

P 1 rnd.

BOTTOM

Pm every 6 sts.

Rnd 1: *K to 2 sts before the marker, k2tog. Rep from * across the rnd. (40 sts)

Rnd 2 and all even rnds: K with no dec.

Rnd 3: Same as rnd 1. (32 sts)

Rnd 5: Same as rnd 1. (24 sts)

Rnd 7: Same as rnd 1. (16 sts)

Rnd 9: *K2tog. Rep from * across the rnd. (8 sts) Break yarn and thread through live sts. Pull tight and work in ends.

Wet-felt basket in a washing machine (page 16). Allow to dry.

BEADED RIM

Depending on the size of the needle, you may need to switch back and forth between the beading needle and the sewing needle. The thread should not be doubled over.

Starting anywhere on the top of the basket, sew threaded needle from the inside to the outside, coming out on the line between the lighter and darker colored yarn. Thread enough beads on the needle to cover both the outside and inside of the rim. Insert needle from the inside to the outside, coming out just to the left of the previous row of beads. Continue in this manner until the entire rim is covered. Tie off thread and bury into the felting.

cookie cutter christmas basket

FINISHED MEASUREMENTS: 7-in. wide by 5-in. high
GAUGE: 5 sts in stockinette using 2 strands = 1 inch

Christmastime is such a wonderful time of year. There is nothing like the crispness in the air as snow gently drifts to the frozen earth. Inside, it is cozy, with a roaring fire in the fireplace; the scent of cookies drifts out from the kitchen to compete with the piney aroma of a freshly cut Christmas tree.

That ideal is not always reality—perhaps this basket will help you envision it as children or grandchildren run wild through the house, and with all the chaos, you forget your cookies that are now burning to a crisp. All I can say is . . . Merry Christmas!

MATERIALS & TOOLS

- 1 skein each Cascade 220 yarn (3½ oz/220 yds), in the following colors:
  - 9484 Stratosphere (color A)
  - 8505 White (color B)
  - 9486 Shamrock (color C)
- U.S. size 5 20-in. circular needles
- U.S. size 5 double-pointed needles
- 2 yds ⅜-in.-wide red ribbon
- Blue sewing thread
- Sewing needle
- Size 6 white glass beads
- 4 tree-shaped metal cookie cutters
- #18 tapestry needle
- Stitch markers

NOTE: Use 2 strands held tog when knitting the basket and 1 strand when doing the duplicate st.

SIDES

Using color A, CO 96 sts onto circular needles. Join into round, making sure not to twist sts.

Rnd 1: Purl.

Rnd 2: Knit.

Rnd 3: Purl.

Rnds 4–24: Knit. Break yarn and join color C.

Rnds 25–28: Knit. Break yarn and join color B.

Rnds 29–37: Knit.

Rnd 38: Purl.

BOTTOM

When there are too few stitches to continue to knit in the round with the circular needles, switch to dpn.

Pm every 12 sts.

Rnd 1: *K to 2 sts before the m, k2tog. Rep from * across the rnd. (88 sts)

Rnd 2 and all even rnds: Knit.

Rnd 3: *K to 2 sts before the m, k2tog. Rep from * across the rnd. (80 sts)

Rnd 5: *K to 2 sts before the m, k2tog. Rep from * across the rnd. (72 sts)

Rnd 7: *K to 2 sts before the m, k2tog. Rep from * across the rnd. (64 sts)

Rnd 9: *K to 2 sts before the m, k2tog. Rep from * across the rnd. (56 sts)

Rnd 11: *K to 2 sts before the m, k2tog. Rep from * across the rnd. (48 sts)

Rnd 13: *K to 2 sts before the m, k2tog. Rep from * across the rnd. (40 sts)

Rnd 15: *K to 2 sts before the m, k2tog. Rep from * across the rnd. (32 sts)

Rnd 17: *K to 2 sts before the m, k2tog. Rep from * across the rnd. (24 sts)

Rnd 19: *K to 2 sts before the m, k2tog. Rep from * across the rnd. (16 sts)

Rnd 21: *K to 2 sts before the m, k2tog. Rep from * across the rnd. (8 sts)

Break yarn and thread through rem sts. Pull tight and work in ends.

FINISHING

Using a single strand of color C and the tapestry needle, duplicate st the trees following the chart (see below). Basket will be held upside down while stitching.

Cut ribbon into 4 14-inch pieces. Insert ribbon around the 11th stockinette st from the top edge and tie on a cookie cutter. Each cookie cutter and ribbon will be separated by 23 sts. Using sewing thread, sew on beads to look like snow.

Tree Duplicate Stitch Chart

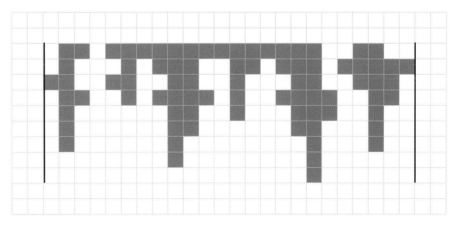

1 SQUARE = 1 STITCH

REPEAT A TOTAL OF 4 TIMES

old glory

FINISHED MEASUREMENTS: 11-in. wide by 4-in. high
GAUGE: 5 sts = 1 inch

One of my favorite movies is *Yankee Doodle Dandy* with James Cagney. Some of you might be reluctant to watch it, because it is in glorious black and white. If you can breech this obstacle, you are in for a wonderful flag-waving treat to America as the movie recounts the life of song writer and entertainer George M. Cohan. Knit this basket as you watch Cagney tap his way across the screen to the title song of the movie. Warning! You might find yourself knitting to the tempo of the music.

MATERIALS & TOOLS

- Berroco Vintage yarn (3½ oz/ 217 yds) in the following colors:
  - 2 skeins 51181 Ruby (color A)
  - 1 skein 5108 Stone (color B)
  - 1 skein 5143 Dark Denim (color C)
- U.S. size 5 needles
- Extra U.S. size 5 needle, any length
- #18 tapestry needle

THREE NEEDLE BIND OFF

With RS tog, insert the third needle into the first st of both needles and k them tog. Rep this on the next first sts. There are now 2 sts on the right needle. Lift the lower or first st over the top or 2nd st and drop off the end of the needle. K the next first sts on the left needle and rep dropping the lower st off the right needle. It is just like a regular BO, except that you are knitting 2 sts tog, 1 from each needle.

NOTE: Hold 2 strands tog throughout.

SIDE 1

CO 60 sts using color A.

Rows 1–4: Sl1 pwise, bring yarn to the back, k to the end. Do not break yarn. Join color B and carry color A loosely along the edge of the knitting.

Rows 5–8: Using color B, sl1 pwise, bring yarn to the back, k to the end. Do not break yarn. Carry color B loosely along the edge of the knitting.

Rows 9–32: Rep rows 1–8 3 times more.

Rows 33–34: Using color A, sl1, k to the end of the row. Break yarn B.

Row 35: Sl1 pwise, p to end of row.

Row 36: Sl1 pwise, k to end of row.

BOTTOM

Slipping the first st pwise on each row and then bringing the yarn to the back, k 36 rows.

SIDE 2

Row 1: Sl1 pwise, p to the end.

Rows 2–4: Sl1 pwise, k to the end. Join color B.

Rows 5–8: Using color B, sl1 pwise, k to the end. Carry color A loosely along the edge of the knitting.

Rows 9–12: Using color A, sl1 pwise, k to the end. Carry color B loosely along the edge of the knitting.

Rows 13–28: Rep rows 5–12 2 times more.

Rows 29–32: Rep rows 5–8 once.

Rows 33–37: Using color A, sl1 pwise, k to the end.

BO.

ENDS

Using color C and with RS facing, pick up and k 54 sts along the short end of basket; pm after the 18th and 36th st.

Row 1: Sl1 pwise, k to the end. (WS)

Row 2: Sl1 pwise, k to 2 sts before the m, ssk, slip m, k2tog, k to 2 sts before the next m, ssk, slip m, k2tog, k to the end. (RS) (50 sts)

Row 3: Same as row 1.

Row 4: Same as row 2. (46 sts)

Row 5: Same as row 1.

Row 6: Same as row 2. (42 sts)

Row 7: Same as row 1.

Row 8: Same as row 2. (38 sts)

Row 9: Same as row 1.

Row 10: Same as row 2. (34 sts)

Row 11: Same as row 1.

Row 12: Same as row 2. (30 sts)

Row 13: Same as row 1.

Row 14: Same as row 2. (26 sts)

Row 15: Same as row 1.

Row 16: Same as row 2. (22 sts)

Row 17: Same as row 1.

Row 18: K9, ssk, k2tog, k9. (20 sts)

Fold knitting with RSs tog. Place 10 sts on 1 needle and 9 sts on another needle. With a 3rd needle, do a 3 needle BO (see page 25).

Rep basket ends on the other end.

BOBBLE

Look at the photo on page 25 for bobble placement. Using color B, make a slipknot and place it on a needle.

Row 1: (K, p, k) into slipknot. Turn.

Row 2: Purl. Turn.

Row 3: Sl2 kwise, k1, pass sl sts over the k st. Cut yarn, leaving a 4-inch tail. Pull tail through rem st.

Using a tapestry needle with tails threaded, sew tails to the back, tie in a square knot, and bring tails out through the bobble. Trim tails. Rep until there are 8 bobbles around the pattern. Rep on the other end of the basket.

fluffy the basket

FINISHED MEASUREMENTS: 5½-in. wide by 3½-in. high (White); 8-in. wide by 4-in. high (Groovy)
GAUGE: 5 sts in stockinette using 2 strands = 1 inch

It might be hard to believe, but when my children were little, they had plastic yard flamingos as pets. For a variety of reasons, actual pets were not in the cards for our family, but our children still have fond memories of Ferdinand and Isabella keeping watch over their mealtimes through a big picture window next to our dining table. If you find yourself desiring a low maintenance "pet" as well, knit up this soft and fluffy basket.

MATERIALS & TOOLS

- For the White variation: 2 skeins Cascade 220 (3½ oz/220 yds) in 8505 White
- For the Feeling Groovy variation: 1 skein Red Heart Super Saver yarn in 3933 Dove; and Red Heart Super Saver yarn, variegated colors of choice
- U.S. size 5 16-in. circular needles
- U.S. size 6 16-in. circular needles
- U.S. size 6 double-pointed needles
- Stitch markers
- Pom-pom maker (such as Pattiewack Mini Pom-Pom Maker)
- Yarn needle

NOTE: Hold 2 strands tog throughout the basket.

White variation has 23 side rounds; Feeling Groovy has 20.

Knitted by Heidi Rietjens.

SIDES

Using U.S. size 5 needles, CO 80 sts. Join into round; do not twist sts.

Rnd 1: Purl.

Rnd 2: Knit.

Rnd 3: Purl. Switch to U.S. size 6 circular needles.

K each rnd until stockinette portion measures 3 inches. P 1 rnd.

BOTTOM

When there are too few sts to cont to k in the round with the circular needles, switch to dpn.

Pm every 10 sts.

Rnd 1: *K to 2 sts before the m, k2tog. Rep from * across the rnd. (72 sts)

Rnd 2 and all even rnds: Knit.

Rnd 3: *K to 2 sts before the m, k2tog. Rep from * across the rnd. (64 sts)

Rnd 5: *K to 2 sts before the m, k2tog. Rep from * across the rnd. (56 sts)

Rnd 7: *K to 2 sts before the m, k2tog. Rep from * across the rnd. (48 sts)

Rnd 9: *K to 2 sts before the m, k2tog. Rep from * across the rnd. (40 sts)

Rnd 11: *K to 2 sts before the m, k2tog. Rep from * across the rnd. (32 sts)

Rnd 13: *K to 2 sts before the m, k2tog. Rep from * across the rnd. (24 sts)

Rnd 15: *K to 2 sts before the m, k2tog. Rep from * across the rnd. (16 sts)

Rnd 17: *K2tog. Rep from * across the rnd. (8 sts)

Break yarn and thread through rem sts. Pull tight and work in ends.

POM-POMS

White Version: Using the pom-pom maker, make 20 2-inch pom-poms and 40 1½-inch pom-poms, leaving long tails.

On the 12th stockinette row, thread one of the tails between 2 sts above the horizontal bar to the inside of the basket. Tie tails tightly. Thread tails back to the front and into the pom-pom; trim the tails to blend in.

Place a 2-inch pom-pom every 4 sts. The smaller pom-poms will be staggered between the larger pom-poms, tying them around the 5th down from the garter stitch edge and the 5th row up from the bottom p row.

Feeling Groovy Variation: Make 2½-, 2-, and 1½-inch pom-poms using different variegated yarns. Tie pom-poms on at random, following the directions for Fluffy the Basket. Make sure to cover the basket completely with pom-poms.

knit-purl–slip stitch basket

FINISHED MEASUREMENTS: 7-in. wide by 3½-in. high
GAUGE: 4½ sts in stockinette stitch = 1 inch

Many knitters are intimidated by color work, such as fair isle and intarsia. It is always a pleasure to introduce these timid knitters to slip stitch knitting, because only 1 color is worked on any round or row. The other tidbit of information I love sharing with the novice knitter is that there are only 2 stitches in knitting: knit and purl. It is rather amazing the things that can be done with the unlimited combinations of these stitches. With all of that in mind, this basket is a tribute to these humble but mighty stitches. And the basket will make a wonderful conversation piece at your next knitting circle.

MATERIALS & TOOLS

- 1 skein each Berroco Vintage yarn (3½ oz/217 yds) in the following colors:
  - 5190 Aubergine (color A)
  - 51168 Petals (color B)
- U.S. size 7 16-in. circular needles
- U.S. size 7 double-pointed needles
- U.S. size 8 straight or circular needles
- Stitch marker

NOTE: To read the chart on page 32, start at the lower right-hand corner. Read the chart from right to left. Each row on the chart represents 2 rnds, with the first of the rnds being a k rnd and the 2nd a p rnd. The color being used for that rnd is in the box next to the row number. K or p the sts shown in the color for the row and slip the other sts pwise. On the p rows, the yarn will have to be brought to the inside of the basket when slipping these sts. Then bring the yarn to the outside when purling the next st of the color being worked.

BOTTOM

With color A, CO 8 sts using the dpn, distributing the sts evenly over 4 needles.

Rnd 1: Join into round, making sure not to twist sts. Knit.

Rnd 2: KFB each st (see page 13). (16 sts)

Rnds 3–5: Knit.

Rnd 6: Same as rnd 2. (32 sts)

Rnds 7–10: Knit.

Rnd 11: Same as rnd 2. (64 sts) Switch to the U.S. size 7 circular needles.

Rnds 12–16: Knit.

Rnd 17: *(K1, kfb) 7 times, k2. Rep from * across the rnd. (92 sts)

Rnds 18–23: Knit.

Rnd 24: Purl. Join color B.

SIDES

Start row 1 of the chart. On the last row of the chart, BO in p using the U.S. size 8 needles. Break yarns and work in ends.

Purl Knit Words Chart

Repeat twice

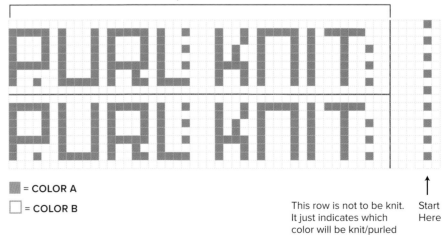

■ = COLOR A

□ = COLOR B

This row is not to be knit. It just indicates which color will be knit/purled

↑ Start Here

faux basketweave basket

FINISHED MEASUREMENTS: 8-in. wide by 6-in. high

GAUGE: 2 sts in stockinette = 1 inch

Like me, I'll bet you had a knitting spool as a child. Perhaps you had a store-bought one, or one fashioned from a wooden thread spool and some nails. Either way, watching the cord grow out the bottom of the spool was very satisfying—up to a point. Soon the question popped into my mind as to what to do with the yards of cord. After the discovery of an automatic spool loom and some beautiful sock yarn, I found I could crank out cord quickly and use it to knit baskets. Now you know what to do with all that I-cord!

MATERIALS & TOOLS

- 6 skeins Brown Sheep Company Wildfoote Luxury Sock Yarn (1¾ oz/215 yds) in Ragtime SY300
- U.S. size 13 double-pointed needles
- U.S. size 13 24-in. circular needles
- Automatic spool loom (such as Embellish-Knit!)
- #18 tapestry needle

I-CORD

Leaving a 4-inch tail and using the automatic spool loom, knit each skein of sock yarn into an I-cord. Sew I-cords tog using the tails at each end to create the I-cord yarn.

SIDES

Using 24-inch circular needles, CO 56 sts.

Rnd 1: *K4, p4. Rep from * across the rnd.

Rnds 2–4: Rep rnd 1.

Rnd 5: *P4, k4. Rep from * across the rnd.

Rnds 6–8: Rep rnd 5.

Rnds 9–16: Rep rnds 1–8.

BOTTOM

Switch to dpn.

Rnd 1: *K5, ssk. Rep from * across the rnd. (48 sts)

Rnd 2: Knit.

Rnd 3: *K4, ssk. Rep from * across the rnd. (40 sts)

Rnd 4: Knit.

Rnd 5: *K3, ssk. Rep from * across the rnd. (32 sts)

Rnd 6: Knit.

Rnd 7: *K2, ssk. Rep from * across the rnd. (24 sts)

Rnd 8: Knit.

Rnd 9: *K1, ssk. Rep from * across the rnd. (16 sts)

Rnd 10: Knit.

Rnd 11: *K2tog. Rep from * across the rnd. (8 sts)

Thread yarn through live sts and pull tight. Work in ends.

chalkboard

FINISHED MEASUREMENTS: 5-in. wide by 4½-in. high
GAUGE: 5 sts in stockinette with 2 strands = 1 inch

It would not be a stretch to say that most teachers have enough coffee mugs to open up a coffee shop. Every year, teachers across the country receive these mugs as tokens of appreciation from sometimes-reluctant students and, of course, their parents. As a fellow knitter, I suggest that your favorite teacher just might enjoy one of the following trio of baskets in lieu of the obligatory coffee mug. Your teacher will thank you.

MATERIALS & TOOLS

- 1 skein each Berroco Vintage yarn (3½ oz/ 217 yds) in the following colors:
  - 5144 Cork (color A)
  - 5145 Cast Iron (color B)
  - 5101 Mochi (color C)
- U.S. size 5 16-in. circular needles
- U.S. size 5 double-pointed needles
- 8 stitch markers
- Yarn needle

NOTE: Hold 2 strands tog throughout. Chart on page 38 is read upside down. To read the chart, start at the lower righthand corner. Read the chart from right to left. Each row on the chart represents 2 rnds with the first of the rnds being a k rnd and the second a p rnd. The color being used for the rnd is in the box next to the row number. K or p the sts shown in the color for the row and slip the other sts pwise. On the p rows, the yarn will have to be brought to the inside of the basket when slipping these sts. Then bring the yarn to the outside when purling the next st of the color being worked.

COMPLETE THE SIDES

Rnd 1: Knit.

Rnd 2: *K1, p1. Rep from * across the rnd.

Rnd 3: *P1, k1. Rep from * across the rnd.

Rnd 4: Same as rnd 2.

Rnd 5: Same as rnd 3.

Rnd 6: Same as rnd 2. Pm every 10 sts. Switch to dpn as needed.

BOTTOM

Rnd 1: *K to 2 sts before the m, k2tog. Rep from * across the rnd. (72 sts)

Rnd 2 and all even rnds: Knit.

Rnd 3: Same as rnd 1. (64 sts)

Rnd 5: Same as rnd 1. (56 sts)

Rnd 7: Same as rnd 1. (48 sts)

Rnd 9: Same as rnd 1. (40 sts)

Rnd 11: Same as rnd 1. (32 sts)

Rnd 13: Same as rnd 1. (24 sts)

Rnd 15: Same as rnd 1. (16 sts)

Rnd 17: *K2tog. Rep from * across the rnd. (8 sts) Break yarn and thread into live sts. Pull tight and work in ends.

SIDES

Start with circular needles. With color A, CO 80 sts.

Rnd 1: *K1, p1. Rep from * across the rnd.

Rnd 2: *P1, k1. Rep from * across the rnd.

Rep rnds 1–2 2 more times. Break yarn and join color B.

K 3 rows.

Follow chart, joining color C. Color C on the chart is black and the background is white. On the basket, the colors are reversed. This is done so that the chart is easier to read.

K 3 rows using color B. Break yarn and join color A.

Alphabet Chart

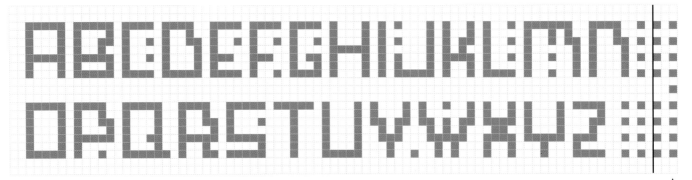

■ = COLOR C

This row is not to be knit. It just indicates which color will be knit/purled

apple for the teacher

FINISHED MEASUREMENTS: 4-in. wide by 4-in. high (excluding stem)
GAUGE: 5 sts in stockinette with 2 strands = 1 inch

Do students ever give their teachers an apple anymore? I wonder where that started in the first place. The association of apples and teachers are forever etched in our minds. Although an apple is certainly a healthier choice, your favorite teacher just might want to fill his or her knitted apple basket with a tempting treat, such as chocolate, to get them through a rough day with their young charges.

MATERIALS & TOOLS

- 1 skein each Berroco Vintage yarn (3½ oz/217 yds) in the following colors:
  - 5150 Berries (color A)
  - 5135 Holly (color B)
  - 5144 Cork (color C)
- U.S. size 5 double-pointed needles
- Size G crochet hook
- Yarn needle

NOTE: Hold 2 strands of yarn tog throughout.

APPLE

Using color A, CO 6 sts onto 1 needle.

Row 1: *KFB. Rep from * to the end of the row. (12 sts) Distribute 12 sts evenly on 4 needles. Join into round, making sure not to twist the sts.

Rnd 2: *KFB, k1. Rep from * across the rnd. (18 sts)

Rnd 3 and all odd rnds to rnd 13: Knit.

Rnd 4: *K1, M1, k2. Rep from * across the rnd. (24 sts)

Rnd 6: *K1, M1, k3. Rep from * across the rnd. (30 sts)

Rnd 8: *K1, M1, k4. Rep from * across the rnd. (36 sts)

Rnd 10: *K1, M1, k5. Rep from * across the rnd. (42 sts)

Rnd 12: *K1, M1, k6. Rep from * across the rnd. (48 sts)

Rnd 14: *K1, M1, k7. Rep from * across the rnd. (54 sts)

Rnds 15–19: Knit.

Rnd 20: Purl.

Rnd 21: Knit.

Rnd 22: Purl.

BO and work in ends.

Make a 2nd apple half, but when 1 st remains, place onto crochet hook.

JOINING APPLE HALVES

Insert hook into the outer loop of the BO edge of the other apple half, yo, and pull through 2 loops. With 1 loop on the hook, *insert hook into the outer loop of the CO edge of both halves, yo, and pull through. Rep from * 7 times more for a total of 9 joins. Break yarn and work in ends.

STEM

Using color C, CO 3 sts. Work I-cord (page 17) for 3 inches. Break yarn and pull through live sts. Work in end on this end of the stem only. Create a large knot in the other end of the I-cord. Insert the end of the I-cord that does not have the knot through the hole at the top of an apple half. The large knot will keep it from pulling through. On the inside, sew stem in place using the tail at that end of the I-cord.

LEAF

Using color B, CO 3 sts.

Row 1: KFB, k1, kfb. (5 sts)

Row 2: Sl1, k to the end.

Row 3: Sl1, kfb, p1, kfb, k1. (7 sts)

Row 4: Same as row 2.

Row 5: Sl1, k2, p1, k3.

Row 6: Same as row 2.

Rows 7–12: Rep rows 5–6 3 times more.

Row 13: Sl1, ssk, p1, k2tog, k1. (5 sts)

Row 14: Same as row 2.

Row 15: SSK, p1, k2tog. (3 sts)

Row 16: Same as row 2.

Row 17: Sl1, k2tog, psso. 1 st rem. Break yarn and pull through rem st. Work in this tail only. Use the other tail to sew leaf to the base of the stem. Make sure that the ridge in the center of the leaf faces up.

tiny pencil

FINISHED MEASUREMENTS: 3-in. wide by 5-in. high
GAUGE: 5 sts in stockinette with 2 strands = 1 inch

This final teacher gift project really dots the *I*s and crosses the *T*s! In honor of the yellow number 2 pencil we've all used throughout school, consider knitting this unmistakable plush version. Though it can't really write, it's sure to have a place of honor on any teacher or writer's desk. You could even change the colors to make a set of bright-tipped markers.

MATERIALS & TOOLS

- 1 skein each Berroco Vintage yarn (3½ oz/217 yds) in the following colors:
  - 5145 Cast Iron (color A)
  - 5104 Mushroom (color B)
  - 5121 Sunny (color C)
  - 5106 Smoke (color D)
  - 51180 Grapefruit (color E)
- U.S. size 5 double-pointed needles
- Stitch markers
- #18 tapestry needle

NOTE: Hold 2 strands of yarn tog throughout.

SIDES

Using color A, CO 24 sts. Distribute evenly between 4 needles. Join into round, making sure not to twist.

Rnd 1: Knit.

Rnds 2–3: Same as rnd 1.

Rnd 4: *K3, M1. Rep from * across the rnd. (32 sts) Break yarn and join color B.

Rnds 5–7: Knit.

Rnd 8: *K4, M1. Rep from * across the rnd. (40 sts)

Rnds 9–11: Knit.

Rnd 12: *K5, M1. Rep from * across the rnd. (48 sts)

Rnds 13–15: Knit. Break yarn and join color C.

Rnds 16–28: *K7, p1. Rep from * across the rnd. Break yarn and join color D.

Rnd 29: Knit.

Rnd 30: Purl.

Rnd 31: Knit.

Rnd 32: Purl. Break yarn and join color E. At this point, using duplicate st, create the number "2" following the chart (at right) in 1 section of the pencil. Skip 2 sections and duplicate st another "2".

Rnds 33–38: Knit. Pm every 6 sts.

BOTTOM

Rnd 1: *K to 2 sts before the m, k2tog. Rep from * across the rnd. (40 sts)

Rnd 2 and all even rnds: Knit.

Rnd 3: Same as rnd 1. (32 sts)

Rnd 5: Same as rnd 1. (24 sts)

Rnd 7: Same as rnd 1. (16 sts)

Rnd 9: *K2tog. Rep from * across the rnd. (8 sts) Break yarn, leaving an 8-inch tail. Thread tail through live sts. Pull tight and work in ends.

Number 2 Chart

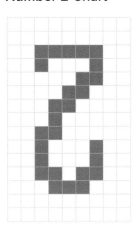

button beauty

FINISHED MEASUREMENTS: 4½-in. wide by 3-in. high

GAUGE: Not applicable due to felting

I once saw a doll that had been completely covered with buttons from head to toe. I marveled at the challenge of sewing those buttons to the tiny form. Inspired by that doll, I thought it would be fun to have a basket embellished with buttons. I have been collecting buttons for a very long time, so it was no problem for me to find both quantity and variety. If your collection of buttons is sparse, consider cruising garage sales, where you can pick up a jar of vintage buttons for a few bucks. The fun will be in selecting which ones to sew to your Button Beauty.

MATERIALS & TOOLS

- 1 skein Cascade 220 yarn (3½ oz/220 yds) in 2424 Summer Night
- U.S. size 9 16-in. circular needles
- U.S. size 9 double-pointed needles
- Vintage buttons
- Sewing thread to match yarn
- Sewing needle
- Stitch markers

Knitted by Leslie Rogers.

SIDES

CO 96 sts. Join into round making sure not to twist sts.

Rnd 1: Purl.

Rnd 2: Knit.

Rnd 3: Purl.

Rnd 4: Knit. Continue knitting every rnd until basket measures 6 inches. Pm every 12 sts.

BOTTOM

When there are too few stitches to continue to knit in the round with the circular needles, switch to dpn.

Rnd 1: *K to 2 sts before the m, k2tog. Rep from * across the rnd. (88 sts)

Rnd 2 and all even rnds: Knit.

Rnd 3: Same as rnd 1. (80 sts)

Rnd 5: Same as rnd 1. (72 sts)

Rnd 7: Same as rnd 1. (64 sts)

Rnd 9: Same as rnd 1. (56 sts)

Rnd 11: Same as rnd 1. (48 sts)

Rnd 13: Same as rnd 1. (40 sts)

Rnd 15: Same as rnd 1. (32 sts)

Rnd 17: Same as rnd 1. (24 sts)

Rnd 19: Same as rnd 1. (16 sts)

Rnd 21: *K2tog. Rep from * across the rnd. (8 sts) Break yarn, leaving an 8-inch tail. Thread through rem sts and pull tight. Work in ends.

FINISHING

Wet-felt basket by placing it in the washing machine until the basket is rigid (page 16). Let dry.

Gather a variety of vintage buttons. Sew buttons closely to each other onto sides of the basket.

noah's ark

FINISHED MEASUREMENTS: 12-in. wide by 5-in. high (excluding rainbow)
GAUGE: 5 sts in stockinette stitch with 2 strands = 1 inch

One of the most beloved stories in the Bible certainly has to be the story of Noah and the ark he built to rescue the animals before the impending flood that was coming. This story has been immortalized in both paintings and children toys. Can't you just picture some small stuffed animals marching up to your ark basket to be safely tucked inside for the night?

MATERIALS & TOOLS

- Brown Sheep Company, Lamb's Pride Bulky yarn (4 oz/125 yds) in the following colors:
  - 2 skeins 151 bulky Chocolate Souffle (color A)
  - 1 skein 02 bulky Brown Heather (color B)
  - 1 skein 197 bulky Red Hot Passion (color C)
  - 1 skein 110 bulky Orange You Glad (color D)
  - 1 skein 155 bulky Lemon Drop (color E)
  - 1 skein 169 bulky Woodland Green (color F)
  - 1 skein 79 bulky Blue Boy (color G)
  - 1 skein 182 bulky Regal Purple (color H)
- U.S. size 5 20-in. circular needles
- Size H crochet hook
- Yarn needle

NOTE: Hold 2 strands of yarn tog throughout.

BOTTOM
CO 6 sts using color A.

Rows 1–3: Sl1 pwise, k to end.

Row 4: Sl1, M1, k to 1 st before the end, M1, k1. (8 sts) (WS)

Rep rows 1–4 until there are 24 sts.

K 36 rows, always slipping the first st.

Next row: Sl1, ssk, k to 3 sts before the end of the row, k2tog, k1. (22 sts)

Next 3 rows: Sl1, k to the end.

Rep these 4 rows until there are 6 sts rem. BO.

SIDE 1
With either side facing, pick up and k 54 sts along on edge of the boat bottom using color B.

Row 1: Sl1, p to the end.

Rows 2–3: Sl1, k to the end. Join color A, but do not break color B.

Rows 4–7: Using color A, sl1, k to the end.

Rows 8–11: Using color B, rep rows 4–7.

Rep rows 4–11 4 times more for a total of 11 stripes. You will always be starting a new color on the WS. K 1 more using color B before binding off. Make sure to slip the first st pwise on this row also. Rep for the other side of the basket.

FRONT
With RS facing and using color A, place slipknot onto needle and pick up 6 sts along the CO edge between basket sides. Then CO 1 st using a knitted CO. (8 sts) Always slipping the first st pwise, k 50 rows. BO. Rep at the other end of the basket.

JOIN SIDES AND ENDS
To join sides to the ends, insert crochet hook in the slipped st on the left side of the end strip and into the slipped sts on the basket side. Make a slip knot using color B and place onto the crochet hook. Pull loop through to the outside. Go up to the next slipped stitch edge and insert crochet hook. YO and pull through both edges. Rep this up the left side of the end piece. Rep on the right edge and then the other end piece. The end pieces will stick up about an inch above the sides of the basket.

RAINBOW HANDLE
Using color C, CO 63 sts.

Row 1: Sl1, k1, *sl1 wyif, bring yarn to the back, k1. Rep from * across the row until there is 1 st rem; k1. (RS)

Row 2: Sl1, p1, *sl1 wyib, bring yarn to the front, p1. Rep from * across the row until there is 1 st rem; p1. (WS)

Row 3: K across the row. Slide yarn to the other end of the needle so that the RS is facing. Break color C and join color D.

Rows 4–6: With color D, rep rows 1–3 1 more time. Break color D and join color E.

Rows 7–9: With color E, rep rows 1–3 1 more time. Break color E and join color F.

Rows 10–12: With color F, rep rows 1–3 1 more time. Break color F and join color G.

Rows 13–15: With color G, rep rows 1–3 1 more time. Break color G and join color H.

Rows 16–18: With color H, rep rows 1–3 1 more time. BO in p. Work in ends. Sew handle to each basket end.

all zipped up

FINISHED MEASUREMENTS: 12-in. wide by 8-in. high
GAUGE: Not applicable due to felting

Have you ever wondered who invented the zipper? We can thank Gideon Sundback for the idea of a continuous fastener back in 1913. B.F. Goodrich Company used the zipper on their manufactured galoshes, and are credited with coining the word "zipper." 1937 saw the "Battle of the Fly" among French fashion designers exploring the idea of zipper versus buttons in men's trousers. In today's fabric stores, one is confronted with all sorts of zippers in a range of colors and lengths. This basket is a nod to those pioneers of the early days of the continuous fastener. The zippers in this basket are more a decorative element than functional, but it sure is fun to zip and unzip them.

MATERIALS & TOOLS

- 1 skein Lion Brand Fishermen's Wool yarn (8 oz/465 yds) in 126 Nature's Brown
- U.S. 10 needles or U.S. 10 16-in. circular needles
- 4 9-in. zippers in different colors
- Thread to match yarn
- Sewing needle
- Stitch marker
- Yarn needle

NOTE: Use a knitted CO throughout.

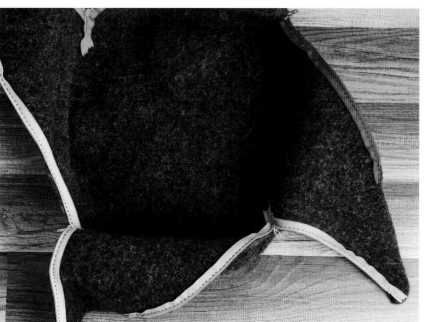

Knitted by Megan Senini.

SQUARES A AND B

CO 69 sts. Mark st 35 with a pm.

Row 1: K to the last st, p. (WS)

Row 2: Sl first st kwise, k to 1 st before the m, sl1, k2tog, psso. Replace pm on center st. K to last st, p. (RS)

Row 3: Sl first st kwise. K to last st, p.

Rep rows 2–3 until 5 sts remain.

Next row: Sl1, sl1, k2tog, psso, p. (RS) (3 sts)

Next row: Sl1, k1, p. (WS)

Next row: Sl1, k2tog, psso. Break yarn, pull through, and work in tail.

SQUARES C AND D

Place squares A and B face up on a flat surface following the illustration (at right). Starting along the left edge of square B, pick up 33 sts. CO 1 st. Pick up 33 sts along the right edge of square A. (67 sts) Follow instructions for knitting squares A and B. Starting along the left edge of square A, pick up 33 sts. Pick up 1 st for the center CO st. Pick up 33 sts along the right edge of square B. (67 sts) Follow instructions for knitting squares A and B.

SIDES

Place squares A, B, C, and D face up on a flat surface following the chart (at right). Pick up 34 sts across the top of square A. Pick up 1 st in the corner. Pick up 34 sts along the right edge of square C. Follow directions for knitting squares A and B, except you will leave the last st on your needle. Pick up 33 more sts across the top of the square just knit. Pick up an extra st in the corner for a total of 35 sts.

TRIANGLE TOP

Row 1: Sl first st kwise. K to last st, p. (WS) (35 sts)

Row 2: Sl first st kwise, k2tog, k to last st, p. (RS) (34 sts)

Rep rows 1–2 until 3 sts remain.

Next row: (WS) Sl1, k1, p1.

Next row: (RS) Sl1 kwise, p2tog. (2 sts)

Next row: (WS) Sl1 kwise, p1.

Last row: Sl1 kwise, k1, psso. Break yarn, pull through, and work in ends.

Placement Illustration

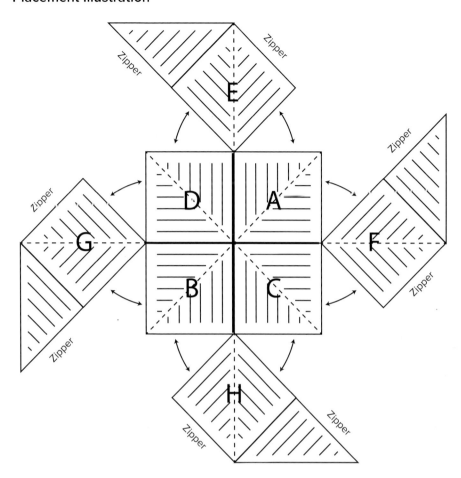

OUTER SQUARES

Pick up 34 sts across the top of square C. Pick up 1 st in the corner. Pick up 34 sts along the right edge of square B. Follow directions for knitting squares A and B, except you will leave the last st on your needle. Pick up 33 more sts across the top of the square just knit. Pick up an extra st in the corner for a total of 35 sts. Follow the directions for the triangle top.

Pick up 34 sts across the top of square B. Pick up 1 st in the corner. Pick up 34 sts along the right edge of square D. Follow directions for knitting squares A and B, except you will leave the last st on your needle. Pick up 33 more sts across the top of the square just knit. Pick up an extra st in the corner for a total of 35 sts. Follow the directions for the triangle top.

Pick up 34 sts across the top of square D. Pick up 1 st in the corner. Pick up 34 sts along the right edge of square A. Follow directions for knitting squares A

and B, except you will leave the last st on your needle. Pick up 33 more sts across the top of the square just knit. Pick up an extra st in the corner for a total of 35 sts. Follow the directions for the triangle top.

FINISHING

Wet-felt piece in the washing machine, making sure to measure the open lengths of the triangles while it is still wet (page 16). Pull into shape as needed, so that each triangle is the correct length. Let dry.

Baste and then sew zippers into diagonal corners.

fish bowl basket

FINISHED MEASUREMENTS: 6-in. high by 9-in. wide
GAUGE: 5 sts = 1 inch

Fish have always been popular in my family. My father loved to fish and also kept pet fish, including a piraña. My love of fish started with catching a hammerhead shark at the age of 4; at 10, I spent months doing odd jobs saving up for my very own aquarium; in college, my pet goldfish Cedric kept me company. As an adult, I discovered several paintings of goldfish bowls by Matisse. These paintings, along with all my scaly encounters, were the inspiration for this basket. The good news is that you don't ever need to feed the fish or clean out the bowl. Yuck!

MATERIALS & TOOLS

- 1 skein each Brown Sheep Company, Lamb's Pride Worsted yarn (4 oz/190 yds) in the following colors:
  - M10 Cream (color A)
  - M285 Frosted Periwinkle (color B)
  - M115 Oatmeal (color C)
  - M110 Orange You Glad (color D)
  - M172 Deep Pine (color E)
- 2 yds black worsted weight yarn, any brand
- U.S. size 6 16-in. circular needles
- U.S. size 6 16-in. double-pointed needles
- Stitch markers
- Yarn needle
- Sewing needle
- Pins
- Orange thread to match
- Size G crochet hook

NOTE: For the fish bowl, hold 2 strands tog throughout. For the goldfish and algae, use a single strand.

BASKET

Using the circular needles and color A, CO 72 sts. Join into round.

Rnds 1–8: Knit.

Rnd 9: *K9, M1, pm. Rep from * across the rnd. (80 sts) Break yarn and join color B.

Rnd 10: Knit.

Rnd 11: *K10, M1. Rep from * across the rnd. (88 sts)

Rnd 12: Knit.

Rnd 13: *K11, M1. Rep from * across the rnd. (96 sts)

Rnds 14–16: Knit.

Rnd 17: *K12, M1. Rep from * across the rnd. (104 sts)

Rnds 18–22: Knit.

Rnd 23: *K13, M1. Rep from * across the rnd. (112 sts)

Rnds 24–36: Knit.

Rnd 37: *K12, ssk. Rep from * across the rnd. (104 sts)

Rnds 38–42: Knit.

Rnd 43: *K11, ssk. Rep from * across the rnd. (96 sts) Break yarn and join color C. Switch to dpn as needed.

Rnds 44–46: Knit.

Rnd 47: *K10, ssk. Rep from * across the rnd. (88 sts)

Rnd 48: Knit.

Rnd 49: *K9, ssk. Rep from * across the rnd. (80 sts)

Rnd 50: Knit.

Rnd 51: *K8, ssk. Rep from * across the rnd. (72 sts)

Rnd 52: Knit.

Rnd 53: *K7, ssk. Rep from * across the rnd. (64 sts)

Rnd 54: Knit.

Rnd 55: *K6, ssk. Rep from * across the rnd. (56 sts)

Rnd 56: Knit.

Rnd 57: *K5, ssk. Rep from * across the rnd. (48 sts)

Rnd 58: Knit.

Rnd 59: *K4, ssk. Rep from * across the rnd. (40 sts)

Rnd 60: Knit.

Rnd 61: *K3, ssk. Rep from * across the rnd. (32 sts)

Rnd 62: Knit.

Rnd 63: *K2, ssk. Rep from * across the rnd. (24 sts)

Rnd 64: Knit.

Rnd 65: *K1, ssk. Rep from * across the rnd. (16 sts)

Rnd 66: Knit.

Rnd 67: *SSK. Rep from * across the rnd. (8 sts) Break yarn, leaving an 8-inch tail. Thread yarn needle with the tail. Run through live rem sts. Pull tight and work in ends.

GOLDFISH

CO 2 sts using 2 dpn and color D.

Rows 1–2: Knit.

Row 3: KFB twice. (4 sts)

Rows 4–5: Knit.

Row 6: K1, kfb twice, k1. (6 sts)

Rows 7–8: Knit.

Row 9: K1, kfb, k2, kfb, k1. (8 sts)

Rows 10–21: Knit.

Row 22: K1, ssk, k2, k2tog, k1. (6 sts)

Rows 23–24: Knit.

Row 25: K1, ssk, k2tog, k1. (4 sts)

Rows 26–27: Knit.

Row 28: K1, kfb twice, k1. (6 sts)

Row 29: Knit.

Row 30: K1, kfb, k2, kfb, k1. (8 sts)

BO loosely. Break yarn and work in ends.

Using the black yarn, make a French knot for the eye, referencing the photo on page 54. Make 7 goldfish or the desired number.

Place goldfish on the bowl and pin in place where desired. Using a sewing needle and orange thread, sew fish by catching the edge of the knitting all around the fish. If you wish for your fish to be in front of the algae, put algae in first.

Using the yarn needle and color A, sew French knots where desired near each fish's mouth for bubbles.

ALGAE

Using color E, make a slipknot and place skein inside fishbowl. With the crochet hook on the outside, insert it into the inside starting somewhere at the bottom in the color C area. Catch slipknot with the crochet hook and bring it to the outside. Reinsert hook ¼-inch above the st on the hook. YO on the inside of the bowl and pull to the outside and through the st on the hook. Rep this, moving hook both up and to the right or left to make wavy algae. When algae is tall enough, cut yarn on inside, making sure there is at least about 3 inches. Pull through to the outside and through the st on the hook. Using a yarn needle, thread tail back to the inside, making sure to tack down the last loop pulled to the front. Work in ends. Surface-crochet algae over fish where desired.

bad hair day

FINISHED MEASUREMENTS: 7-in. wide by 7-in. high
GAUGE: 3 sts = 1 inch

You know it is concerning when even your own mother tells you that you have bad hair. Granted, she just confirmed what I already knew, but it was startling to hear it from her. This basket is dedicated to the bad hair days we all have from time to time, but especially for those of you who are in a perpetual state of bad hair despite all of your efforts, like me.

MATERIALS & TOOLS

- 1 skein Red Heart Super Saver yarn (7 oz/364 yds) in 312 Black
- Stash of yarns, any weight, color, or texture will work
- U.S. size 9 double-pointed needles
- U.S. size 9 16-in. circular needles
- 8 stitch markers
- Size H crochet hook

NOTE: Hold 2 strands tog throughout.

Knitted by Leslie Rogers.

BOTTOM

When there are too few sts to continue to knit in the round with the circular needles, switch to dpn. CO 8 sts and distribute them over 4 needles.

Rnd 1: Join into round, making sure not to twist the sts. K.

Rnd 2: *K1, M1, pm. Rep from * across the rnd. (16 sts)

Rnd 3: Knit.

Rnd 4: *K to pm, M1, slip pm. Rep from * across the rnd. (24 sts)

Rnd 5: Knit.

Rep rnds 4–5 until the bottom measures 7 inches, increasing 8 sts every other row.

SIDES

Rnd 1: *K1, bring yarn to the front, sl1, bring yarn to the back. Rep from * across the rnd ending with a sl1.

Rnd 2: Knit.

Rnd 3: *Bring yarn to the front, sl1, bring yarn to the back, k1. Rep from * across the rnd ending with a k1.

Rnd 4: Knit.

Rep rnds 1–4 until the desired height is reached.

K 11 rnds more. BO loosely or use a needle one size larger.

EMBELLISHMENT

Starting at the bottom, insert a crochet hook into 1 of the sl st loops going from top to bottom. Fold a piece of novelty yarn 6 inches long in half. Pull this partway through the loop on the basket. Using the crochet hook, pull the ends through the loop of novelty yarn. Tighten by hand. Rep this in all the loops, working 1 rnd at a time from the bottom of the basket up toward the top.

plastic bag solution basket

FINISHED MEASUREMENTS: 9-in. wide by 6-in. high
GAUGE: 3 sts in stockinette = 1 inch

Most of us get a few plastic bags every week. We may keep some to use again, or we may throw them out. As we multiply this by each family, we are talking about a great deal of plastic bags. Here is a solution to help keep those bags out of the landfill—just knit a basket out of them. Make some for friends and family. Won't it feel good knowing that you were able to keep a few more plastic bags out of the dump?

MATERIALS & TOOLS

- 1 skein Red Heart Super Saver yarn (7 oz/364 yds) in 312 Black
- Approx 50 plastic grocery bags
- U.S. size 10½ 24-inch circular needles
- U.S. size 10½ 16-inch circular needles
- U.S. size 10½ double-pointed needles
- Stitch markers
- Yarn needle

NOTE: Hold plastic yarn tog with 1 strand of the black yarn throughout.

PLASTIC BAG PREPARATION

Flatten bags one at a time. Cut the bottom and handles of the bag off. Cut 2-inch strips starting at the bottom from 1 side of the bag to the other. You should get approx 5 strips per bag. If you are using more than 1 color, toss the grocery bag loops like a salad. To loop tog, insert 1 loop into another. Insert 1 end of the first loop through the other end of that loop. Gently pull tight. Continue to join grocery bag loops tog. Roll into a ball.

SIDES

Using the larger size circular needles, CO 72 sts. Join into round without twisting the sts.

Rnd 1: Purl.

Rnd 2: Knit.

Rnd 3: Purl.

Rnd 4: Knit.

Continue to k every rnd until basket measures 6 inches from the beginning.

BOTTOM

When there are too few stitches to continue to knit in the round with the smaller circular needles, switch to dpn. Pm every 9 sts.

Rnd 1: *K7, ssk. Rep from * across the rnd. (64 sts)

Rnd 2: Knit.

Rnd 3: *K6, ssk. Rep from * across the rnd. (56 sts)

Rnd 4: Knit.

Rnd 5: *K5, ssk. Rep from * across the rnd. (48 sts)

Rnd 6: Knit.

Rnd 7: *K4, ssk. Rep from * across the rnd. (40 sts)

Rnd 8: Knit.

Rnd 9: *K3, ssk. Rep from * across the rnd. (32 sts)

Rnd 10: Knit.

Rnd 11: *K2, ssk. Rep from * across the rnd. (24 sts)

Rnd 12: Knit.

Rnd 13: *K1, ssk. Rep from * across the rnd. (16 sts)

Rnd 14: Knit.

Rnd 15: SSK across the rnd. (8 sts) Break yarns, leaving a 10-inch tail. Thread yarns through live sts and pull tight. Work in ends.

zoetrope

FINISHED MEASUREMENTS: 8-in. wide by 3½-in. high
GAUGE: 4 sts = 1 inch

The zoetrope originated with the Victorians and was also popular with the Surrealists. A precursor to film animation, it produced the illusion of motion by displaying either drawings or photographs in a progressive sequence. Viewers would watch the motion through slits on the outside as the zoetrope was spun. This basket creates visual motion: your vision tends to first notice warm colors, such as the orange in this basket, and then go to the cooler colors. You may not be conscious of it, but for most people, this what your eye will do. There are three other variations of this project; see the instructions that follow.

MATERIALS & TOOLS

- 1 skein each Red Heart Super Saver yarn (7 oz/364 yds) in the following colors:
  - 256 Carrot (color A)
  - 656 Real Teal (color B)
  - 776 Dark Orchid (color C)
- U.S. size 9 16-in. circular needles
- U.S. size 9 double-pointed needles
- Size I crochet hook
- Interchangeable knitting needle set (such as Denise), which can be used as a stitch holder
- Yarn needle

NOTE: Hold 2 strands of yarn tog throughout.

Row 3: Sl1 pwise, bring yarn to the back, k6, sl next st kwise, insert needle into next loop on the right edge of the previous strip. Pick up and k 1 st and pass the slipped st over this picked up st. Turn work. (RS)

Continue to rep rows 2–3 until a total of 28 rows have been knitted, ending with a RS row. On the last pick up and k row, pick up the st by going into the knot at the top of the previous k strip.

The next strip will be knit using color C. Continue knitting strips in the color order until there are 12 strips. This last strip will only be attached to the strip to its left. To join the final 2 strips tog, using color B, make a slipknot. Hold the slipknot inside the basket. With the RS facing, insert the crochet hook into the knitting at the base of the first strip knitted. Then insert the hook in the last strip knitted and pull through the slipknot to the front. With 1 loop on the hook, insert the hook to the inside of the basket by first inserting it in the top 2 strands of the edge st on the right and then into the 2 top strands of the left strip edge st. YO and pull to the front and through the loop on the hook. Continue chaining upward until the 2 strips are joined. Break yarn and work in ends.

BOTTOM

Using color B on the dpn, CO 8 sts. Distribute over 4 needles.

Rnd 1: Join into round, making sure not to twist the sts; k.

Rnd 2: KFB in each st. (16 sts)

Rnds 3–5: Knit.

Rnd 6: Same as rnd 2. (32 sts)

Rnds 7–10: Knit.

Rnd 11: Same as rnd 2. (64 sts)

Rnds 12–16: Knit.

Rnd 17: *K1, kfb. Rep from * across the rnd. (96 sts)

Rnds 18–23: Knit.

SIDES

Put all sts except the 8 sts that would be knit next on the interchangeable set's cable.

K every row for 28 rows, always slipping the first st pwise, bringing the yarn to the back after slipping. BO.

Put the next 8 sts to the right of the strip just knit on your working needles.

Row 1: Sl1 (this will be color B), joining color A, k6, sl next st kwise; insert needle into the first loop on the right edge of the previous strip. This will be at the very base. Pick up and k 1 st and pass the sl st over this picked up st. Turn work. (RS)

Row 2: Sl1 pwise, bring yarn to the back. K to the end. (WS)

Show Your Colors Variation

Follow directions for the main version with these changes:

- 1 skein Red Heart Super Saver yarn (7 oz/364 yds) in each of the following colors:
  - 387 Soft Navy (color A)
  - 319 Cherry Red (color B)
  - 316 Soft White (color C)

Use color A for the bottom. Put all but 16 sts on the interchangeable knitting needle set, such as Denise. The strips will be 16 sts wide instead of 8, and there will be 30 rows instead of 28. Knit the first section using color A. Next knit the striped strips, starting with 2 rows of color B, then 2 rows of color C; continue by repeating 2 rows of each. End with color B on rows 29 and 30. Repeat around the sides so each color A section is followed by a striped section.

Weave stars as per instructions provided with the loom, such as the Dewberry Ridge Star Li'l Weaver Pin Loom. Sew stars onto color A strips with sewing thread.

Mondrian Variation

Follow the directions for the main version with these changes:

Reference the pattern at right for color use.

- 1 skein Red Heart Super Saver yarn (7 oz/364 yds) in each of the following colors:
  - 312 Black (color A)
  - 316 Soft White (color B)
  - 319 Cherry Red (color C)
  - 324 Bright Yellow (color D)
  - 385 Royal (color E)
- Size 9 and 10 interchangeable knitting needles (such as Denise) with different length cables

Create the basket bottom using instructions from the main version with color A. For basket sides, follow the charts at right, reading odd rows from right to left and even rows from left to right. You will be knitting one vertical strip at a time. Do not BO; put completed strip on a long interchangeable knitting needle cable. K the next strip. Place on same cable as the first strip. Using color A, join strips as for main version. Continue knitting strips and joining around the basket. Rep the 3 strips on the chart 3 times in order. When the last strip is knit, join on both sides of the strip. Put size 9 needles onto the cable holding the live stitches. K 1 row using color A. Put size 10 needles on cable. BO in p. Work in ends.

NOTE: Hold 2 strands tog throughout. Always slip the first st pwise on each row and bring yarn to back; also do when working side strips of basket. When changing colors, sl first st and bring tail to back. Join new color and k rest of row.

MONDRIAN COLOR BLOCKS CHART

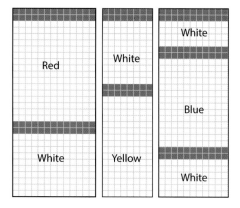

Heartland Variation

Follow directions for the main version with these changes:

- 1 skein Red Heart Super Saver yarn (7 oz/364 yds) in each of the following colors:
    - 387 Soft Navy (color A)
    - 319 Cherry Red (color B)
    - 776 Dark Orchid (color C)
    - 256 Carrot (color D)
    - 656 Real Teal (color E)
    - 376 Burgundy (color F)
    - Heart loom, such as Dewberry Ridge Li'l Weaver Heart Loom
    - Thread to match each yarn

The strips will be 16 sts wide instead of 8 sts. This means there will only be 6 strips. The color order is as follows: A, B, C, D, E, F.

Weave one heart in each color as per instructions provided with the loom.

Sew hearts onto strips using sewing thread. Place each heart on the color strip before that heart's color. For example, the color A strip will have a color B heart.

pinwheel basket

FINISHED MEASUREMENTS: 8-in. wide by 5-in. high

GAUGE: Not applicable due to felting

The first appearance of a pinwheel was in 19th century Redding, California, where a young woman conceived of a wind-driven toy held high by running children. A toy manufacturer in early 20th century Boston refined the toy to its present form. Pinwheels are really quite simple to create, only requiring some heavy paper, a stick, a tack, and of course . . . a little wind. Our knitted tribute to this simple toy won't twirl in the wind, but captures the simple pleasures of childhood in adult form.

MATERIALS & TOOLS

- 1 skein each Cascade 220 yarn (3½ oz/220 yds) in the following colors:
  - 8895 Christmas Red (color A)
  - 9542 Blaze (color B)
  - 7828 Neon Yellow (color C)
  - 8894 Christmas Green (color D)
  - 9484 Stratosphere (color E)
  - 9570 Concord Grape (color F)
- U.S. size 10 16-in. circular needles
- U.S. size 10 24-in. circular needles
- Removable stitch marker
- #18 tapestry needle

NOTE: Use a knitted CO throughout the basket.

PLACEMENT ILLUSTRATION

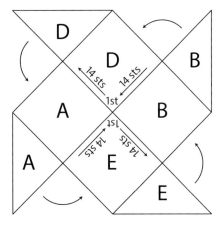

Using tapestry needle, sew triangle A to the edge of square E, triangle E to the edge of square B, triangle B to the edge of square D, and triangle D to the edge of square A.

SIDES

Using color C and 24-inch circular needles, pick up and k 92 sts around the top edge of the pinwheel. You will pick up 23 sts along the edge of each color triangle.

Join into round and k 6 rnds in color C. Break yarn and join color F.

K 6 rnds of color F. Break yarn and join color C.

K 12 rnds in color C. Break yarn and join color F.

Using a knitted CO, CO 3 sts. Continuing with color F, knit an I-cord BO (see page 15) to last 3 sts. BO. Sew I-cord tog. Work in all ends.

Wet-felt as desired (page 16).

BOTTOM

CO 45 sts using color A with 16-inch circular needles.

Row 1: K to the last st, p. (WS) Pm on st 23.

Row 2: Sl first st kwise. K to 1 st before the m. Sl1, k2tog, psso. Replace pm on center st. K to the last st, p. (RS) (43 sts)

Row 3: Sl the first st kwise. K to last st, p.

Rep rows 2–3 until 5 sts remain.

Next row: Sl1, sl1, k2tog, psso, p. (RS) (3 sts)

Next row: Sl1, k1, p. (WS)

Next row: Sl1, k2tog, psso. 1 st remains.

With RS facing, pick up 21 sts along the top of the square and 1 st around the corner for a total of 23 sts.

SQUARE AND TRIANGLE

Row 1: Sl the first st kwise. K to the last st, p. (WS) (23 sts)

Row 2: Sl the first st kwise. K2tog, k to the last st, p. (RS) (21 sts)

Rep rows 1–2 until 3 sts remain.

Next row: Sl1, k1, p1. (WS)

Next row: Sl1 kwise, p2tog. (RS) (2 sts)

Next row: Sl1 kwise, p1. (WS)

Last row: Sl1 kwise, k1, psso. Break yarn, leaving a 12-inch tail for sewing bottom.

Rep square and triangle directions using color B. You will then have 2 pieces that are made up of a square and a triangle. You will now join the bottom using colors D and E.

Referring to the chart (at right), place the color A and B shapes on a flat surface, making sure RSs are facing. Using color D, pick up and k 22 sts along the edge of square color B, CO 1 st, and pick up and k 22 sts along the edge of square color A. (42 sts) With color D, follow the directions for square and triangle.

Using color E, pick up and k 22 sts along the edge of shape A. Pick up 1 st in the CO st, and pick up and k 22 sts along the edge of shape B. With color E, follow directions for square and triangle.

extraterrestrial

FINISHED MEASUREMENTS: 5½-in. wide by 3-in. high
GAUGE: 4 sts in garter stitch = 1 inch

This glow-in-the-dark yarn inspired me to design an extraterrestrial basket. Maybe it was because of all those wonderfully awful black-and-white sci-fi films from the 1950s. There often was some mysterious glowing object that confounded the populace of a remote desert community, usually followed by an invasion of hostile aliens. Ultimately, the Earthlings would prevail. Grab your family and a bowl of popcorn, charge up your glow-in-the-dark basket, and watch a great old sci-fi movie. Don't forget to turn the lights out to enjoy the glow of your basket. Perhaps it's signaling some alien life form—watch out.

MATERIALS & TOOLS

- 1 skein each Yummy Yarns Jelly Yarn, bulky (6 oz/65 yds), in the following colors:
  - Vanilla Peppermint Glow (color A)
  - Green Peppermint Glow (color B)
- 5 U.S. size 8 double-pointed metal needles
- Hand lotion
- Stitch markers
- Cyanoacrylate glue

NOTE: The chart will always be read from right to left. Each row on the chart represents 2 rows of knitting. Look at the color key below the chart to see which color to knit. First, there will be a row of knitting, and then a row of purling. On the first row of a color on the chart, k all the sts of that color and sl all the sts of the other color. On the 2nd row of a color, p. Make sure to bring the yarn to the back before slipping the sts of the other color. Bring yarn back to the front to p. When adding color B for the sl st portion of the basket, make sure to tie a good square knot. When the basket is finished, work in the ends and apply a dot of glue to keep it from unraveling. At the end of the chart section, cut color B and tie off as above.

Rnd 1: *K7, k2tog. Rep from * across the rnd. (64 sts)

Rnd 2 and all even rnds: Knit.

Rnd 3: *K6, k2tog. Rep from * across the rnd. (56 sts)

Rnd 5: *K5, k2tog. Rep from * across the rnd. (48 sts)

Rnd 7: *K4, k2tog. Rep from * across the rnd. (40 sts)

Rnd 9: *K3, k2tog. Rep from * across the rnd. (32 sts)

Rnd 11: *K2, k2tog. Rep from * across the rnd. (24 sts)

Rnd 13: *K1, k2tog. Rep from * across the rnd. (16 sts)

Rnd 15: *K2tog. Rep from * across the rnd. (8 sts)

Cut yarn and thread through rem sts. Pull tight and tie off. Work in ends and apply a dot of glue.

ET LETTERS CHART

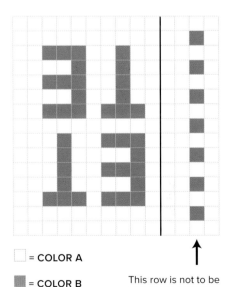

= COLOR A

= COLOR B

This row is not to be knit. It just indicates which color will be knit/purled

SIDES

With color A, CO 72 sts, distributing them evenly over 4 needles, knitting with a 5th needle. Make sure to tie the yarn in a good square knot after the last st is cast on. Later ends can be worked in and a dot of glue applied to keep the knot from coming undone.

Row 1: Purl.

Row 2: Knit.

Row 3: Purl.

Row 4: Start following the chart. It will be rep 9 times total.

Be sure to k 1 row, p 1 row, k 1 row, p 1 row, until complete.

BOTTOM

Pm every 9 sts.

FINISHING

To block, put into a dryer for 5 minutes. Place a cylindrical item inside the basket until the basket cools.

To charge the glow-in-the-dark yarn, expose to bright light.

tie-dyed lotus

MEDIUM

FINISHED MEASUREMENTS: 5-in. wide by 3-in. high
GAUGE: Not applicable due to felting

Have you ever lusted after a yarn you've seen? Was it love at first sight, and you knew you had to use it somehow? I must confess to this with some yarn that my daughter dyed using food coloring.

My prototype used some patriotic hand-dyed yarn I had picked up somewhere along the way, but was now unavailable. Although I hadn't planned on including this basket in the book, I had such an overwhelming response from students that I should. That yarn I had fallen in love with was the perfect replacement. Thus the red, white, and blue became the Tie-Dyed Lotus.

MATERIALS & TOOLS

- 1 skein Lion Brand Fishermen's Wool yarn (8 oz/465 yds) in 123 Oatmeal

- U.S. size 10 16-in. circular needles

- Yarn needle

- Large cooking pot

- 3 packages purple-colored powered drink mix (such as Kool-Aid Grape)

- 2 packages turquoise-colored powered drink mix (such as Kool-Aid Mixed Berry)

- Food coloring of choice

- Small cups

- 9 x 13-in. glass pan

- Eye dropper

- Spray bottle

- White vinegar

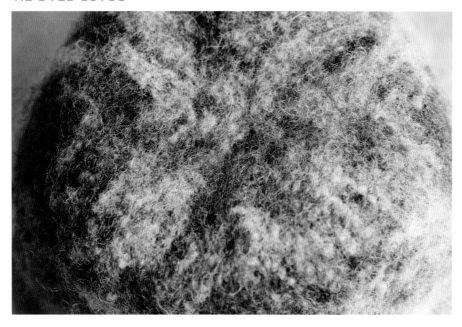

DYEING THE YARN

Skein the yarn into 2 100-yard skeins and 1 200-yard skein. Soak in cold water. Carefully, squeeze out excess water.

Pour 3 quarts of water into a large cooking pot. Add purple drink mix and stir. Turn heat on stove top to medium. Place 1 of the 100-yard skeins into the pot. Bring dye to a simmer. When all of the dye is taken up into the yarn, or when desired color is reached, turn off heat and let cool. Rinse yarn.

Rep, using the turquoise drink mix with the other 100-yard skein.

Select as many food coloring colors as desired and mix a few drops of each color with a few tablespoons of water in small cups. Do not overdilute. Lay the pre-soaked 200-yard skein in a glass 9 x 13-inch pan. Use an eye dropper to drop the different colors all over the skein. Flip the skein over and rep with the dropper and dye. Spray with a 50 / 50 mixture of white vinegar and water. Place in microwave; cook on high power for 90 seconds. Flip the skein over and cook once again for 90 seconds. Let cool and dry.

SQUARES A AND B

Using the multi-colored dyed yarn, CO 27 sts. Mark st 14 with a pm.

Row 1: K to the last st, p. (WS)

Row 2: Sl first st kwise, k to 1 st before the m, sl1, k2tog, psso. Replace pm on center st. K to last st, p. 2 sts decreased. (RS)

Row 3: Sl first st kwise. K to last st, p.

Rep rows 2–3 until 13 rows have been knit. Break yarn and k with the purple dyed yarn. Continue until 5 sts remain.

Assembly Chart

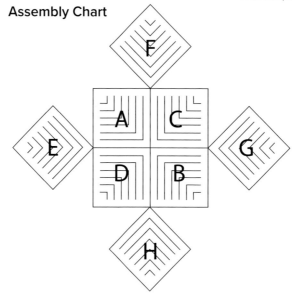

Next row: Sl1, sl1, k2tog, psso, p. (RS) (3 sts)

Next row: Sl1, k1, p. (WS)

Next row: Sl1, k2tog, psso. Break yarn, pull through, and work in tail.

SQUARES C AND D

Place squares A and B face up on a flat surface following the chart (at right). For square C, pick up and k 13 sts along the left CO edge of square B. CO 1 st. Pick up and k 13 sts along the right CO edge of square A. (27 sts) Follow instructions for knitting squares A and B.

For square D, pick up and k 13 sts along the left CO edge of square A. Pick up and k 1 st from the center CO st. Pick up and k 13 sts along the right CO edge of square B. (27 sts) Follow instructions for knitting squares A and B.

SQUARE E

Place squares A, B, C, and D face up on a flat surface according to the chart. For square E, pick up and k 13 sts across the left top edge of square A. Pick up 1 st in the corner. Pick up 13 sts along the right top edge of square D. Follow directions for knitting squares A and B, except use turquoise yarn where purple is indicated.

SQUARES F, G, AND H

Following the directions for square E, knit squares F, G, and H. Use chart for placement.

Wet-felt piece (page 16).

pick, pluck, strum basket

FINISHED MEASUREMENTS: 7-in. wide by 3¾-in. high
GAUGE: 4½ sts with 2 strands = 1 inch

Each of us has gifts and talents. On the flip side, there are some things we just are not equipped to do well. In my case, I don't have a talent for music. I started out with the French horn in 3rd grade; after a semester of mastering only the B flat, my teacher gently suggested that my talents lay elsewhere. The guitar was another failed attempt. As much as I loved guitar music, I didn't even get as far as I did with the French horn. I may have flunked Guitar 101, but I found an artistic use for guitar picks—with a guitar pick punch, I have been embellishing my projects with splashes of color punched from plastic cards.

MATERIALS & TOOLS

- 1 skein Red Heart Super Saver yarn (7 oz/364 yds) in 3933 Dove
- U.S. size 6 double-pointed needles
- U.S. size 6 24-in. circular needles
- Guitar pick punch
- Size E crochet hook
- 50 7mm jump rings
- 50 6mm split rings
- Jewelry pliers
- 12 plastic gift cards or old credit cards
- Drill and small twist bit, or an awl
- Yarn needle

NOTE: Hold 2 strands of yarn throughout.

PREPARING THE GUITAR PICKS

Punch out 4 guitar picks per plastic card. Drill a hole at the top triangular point of the picks. Open up the jump rings with the jewelry pliers and insert a split ring and guitar pick into the jump ring. Close jump ring with pliers. Make 48. There are 24 in each row of picks.

BOTTOM

CO 8 sts onto dpn, distributing evenly over 4 needles.

Rnd 1: Join into round, making sure not to twist the sts. Knit.

Rnd 2: KFB each st. (16 sts)

Rnds 3–5: Knit.

Rnd 6: Same as rnd 2. (32 sts)

Rnds 7–10: Knit.

Rnd 11: Same as rnd 2. (64 sts)

Rnds 12–16: Knit.

Rnd 17: *K1, kfb. Rep from * across the rnd. (96 sts)

Rnds 18–23: Knit.

Switch to circular needles.

Rnd 24: Purl.

SIDES

Rnds 1–10: Knit.

Rnd 11: *K3; place split ring and pick onto the crochet hook. Hook the next st on the left needle and pull through the split ring. Place st back onto the left needle and k the st. Rep from * across the rnd.

Rnd 12: Purl.

Rnds 13–22: Knit.

Rnd 23: K1; *place split ring and pick onto the crochet hook. Hook the next st on the left needle and pull through the split ring. Place st back onto the left needle and k the st. K3. Rep from * until 3 sts are left on the rnd. Add a guitar pick to the next st, k2.

Rnd 24: Purl.

Rnd 25: Knit.

Rnd 26: Purl.

BO with k st. Break yarn and work in ends.

folk art basket

FINISHED MEASUREMENTS: 8-in. wide by 4¼-in. high
GAUGE: 5½ sts = 1 inch

Stranded knitting has a rich tradition in Scandinavia and the British Isles. Hats, mittens, socks, vests, and sweaters sport bands of decorative and whimsical designs. This basket captures a little flavor of those intrepid knitters who have created such functional and beautiful outerwear over the centuries.

MATERIALS & TOOLS

- 1 skein each Berroco Vintage yarn (3½ oz/218 yds) in the following colors:
  - 5150 Berries (color A)
  - 5101 Mochi (color B)
- U.S. size 4 16-in. circular needles
- U.S. size 5 16-in. circular needles
- U.S. size 5 double-pointed needles
- Stitch markers
- Yarn needle

Knitted by Megan Senini.

Folk Art Chart

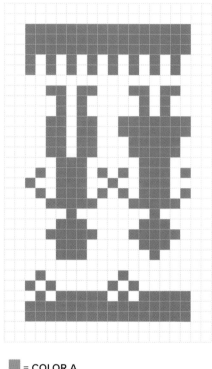

■ = COLOR A

□ = COLOR B

INNER LINING

With color A and using the U.S. size 4 16-inch circular needles, CO 128 sts and join into round, making sure not to twist the sts.

Rnd 1: Purl.

Rnd 2: Knit.

Rnd 3: Purl.

K 26 rows more.

PICOT EDGING

Switching to U.S. size 5 16-inch circular needles, *k2tog, yo. Rep from * across the rnd.

SIDES

Begin following the chart (at top); join color B when needed. Rep 8 times until the sides are complete.

BOTTOM

Pm every 16 sts.

Rnd 1: *K to 2 sts before pm, k2tog. Rep from * across the rnd. (120 sts)

Rnd 2 and all even rnds: Knit.

Rnd 3: *K to 2 sts before pm, k2tog. Rep from * across the rnd. (112 sts)

Rnd 5: *K to 2 sts before pm, k2tog. Rep from * across the rnd. (104 sts)

Rnd 7: *K to 2 sts before pm, k2tog. Rep from * across the rnd. (96 sts)

Rnd 9: *K to 2 sts before pm, k2tog. Rep from * across the rnd. (88 sts)

Rnd 11: *K to 2 sts before pm, k2tog. Rep from * across the rnd. (80 sts)

Rnd 13: *K to 2 sts before pm, k2tog. Rep from * across the rnd. (72 sts)

Rnd 15: *K to 2 sts before pm, k2tog. Rep from * across the rnd. (64 sts)

Rnd 17: *K to 2 sts before pm, k2tog. Rep from * across the rnd. (56 sts)

Rnd 19: *K to 2 sts before pm, k2tog. Rep from * across the rnd. (48 sts)

Rnd 21: *K to 2 sts before pm, k2tog. Rep from * across the rnd. (40 sts)

Rnd 23: *K to 2 sts before pm, k2tog. Rep from * across the rnd. (32 sts)

Rnd 25: *K to 2 sts before pm, k2tog. Rep from * across the rnd. (24 sts)

Rnd 27: *K to 2 sts before pm, k2tog. Rep from * across the rnd. (16 sts)

Rnd 29: *K2tog. Rep from * across the rnd. (8 sts) Break yarn, leaving an 8-inch tail; thread into yarn needle and pull through rem sts. Work in tails.

life savers looper basket

FINISHED MEASUREMENTS: 9-in. wide by 7-in. high
GAUGE: 2 sts in stockinette stitch = 1 inch

Sometimes it's the littlest of things that can mentally transport you back to another time. In my case, that is certainly true of Life Savers candies. Our beloved Great Aunt Ella always had a pack of them around. If we did run out, it meant a short hike to the local store to replenish the stock. It was Aunt Ella who started me on the path of knitting at the tender age of 4. This basket is a tribute to her generosity, both with her Life Savers and her fiber arts talents.

MATERIALS & TOOLS

- 2 16-oz bags Wool Novelty Company cotton blend weaving loops in dark assortment
- U.S. size 13 24-in. circular needles
- U.S. size 13 double-pointed needles
- Stitch markers
- Sewing needle
- Thread to match the orange loops
- Yarn needle

NOTE: Change colors somewhere around the beginning of the rnd. Sometimes it will be right before and sometimes a st or two after the beginning.

CREATING THE LOOPY YARN

Divide loops by color. Place the blue, brown, and black loops tog as 1 color (this will be called the dark-colored mix). Also make piles of orange, green, red, and yellow. Make loopy yarn from each color by inserting 1 loop into another. Then insert that loop into itself and pull tight. Start by making about 2 yards of orange loopy yarn. Add more loops of that color as needed.

SIDES

Using orange, CO 48 sts.

Rnd 1: Purl.

Rnd 2: Knit.

Rnd 3: Purl. Switch to dark-colored mix.

Rnds 4–6: Knit. Switch to green.

Rnd 7: Knit.

Rnd 8: Purl.

Rnd 9: Knit.

Rnd 10: Purl. Switch to dark-colored mix.

Rnds 11–13: Knit. Switch to red.

Rnd 14: Knit.

Rnd 15: Purl.

Rnd 16: Knit.

Rnd 17: Purl. Switch to dark-colored mix.

Rnds 18–20: Knit. Switch to yellow.

Rnd 21: Knit.

Rnd 22: Purl.

Rnd 23: Knit.

Rnd 24: P; pm every 6 sts.

BOTTOM

Rnd 25: *K to 2 sts before the m, ssk. Rep from * across the rnd. (40 sts)

Rnd 26: Knit. Switch to red.

Rnd 27: Rep row 25. (32 sts)

Rnd 28: Knit. Switch to green.

Rnd 29: Rep row 25. (24 sts)

Rnd 30: Knit. Switch to orange.

Rnd 31: Rep row 25. (16 sts)

Rnd 32: Knit.

Rnd 33: *SSK. Rep from * across the rnd. (8 sts)

Pull loop yarn through rem sts and pull tight. Work in ends and sew down with sewing thread.

exotic

FINISHED MEASUREMENTS: 5-in. wide by 3-in. high
GAUGE: 5 sts in stockinette using 2 strands = 1 inch

Gandhi led by example. He encouraged the belief among the people of India that there was dignity in working with their hands. Daily, he would spin some yarn, as did his followers. Eventually, cloth production helped India to gain its independence and create its own economy. The flag of India has the spinning wheel on it as a daily reminder to its populace. India continues to have a reputation for beautiful hand-embroidered textiles. Their imperfections only make them more beautiful, compared with machine-made items. This basket embodies the hand-fashioned beauty of exotic India.

MATERIALS & TOOLS

- 1 skein each Cascade 220 yarn (3½ oz/220 yds) in the following colors:
  - 7827 Goldenrod (color A)
  - 2433 Pacific (color B)
  - 8885 Dark Plum (color C)
- U.S. size 5 16-in. circular needles
- U.S. size 5 double-pointed needles
- Stitch markers
- White glue
- 8 1-in. mirrors (such as Lacis HL55)
- Sewing needle
- 1 skein DMC Pearl Cotton Variations embroidery thread (27 yds, size 5) in color 4210
- Yarn needle

NOTE: Hold 2 strands of yarn tog throughout the basket.

SHISHA EMBROIDERY

Glue mirrors in place on the color B portion of the basket, spacing them out evenly. Allow to dry completely. Using 45 inches of thread for each mirror, follow the directions (page below) for embroidering the mirror in place.

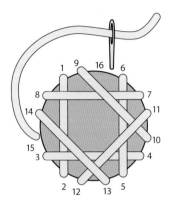

Sew down each mirror by making the stitches as shown from 1 to 2, 3 to 4, etc.

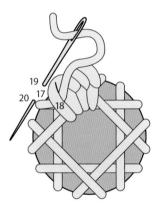

To make the decorative frame stitching, come up at 17 and insert the needle under the stitches from the center out. Draw the needle to the right side of the working thread at 18. Make a stitch from 18 to 19 and come up at 20. Repeat. This is a buttonhole stitch all the way around the mirror.

SIDES

Using color A, CO 64 sts and join into round, making sure not to twist sts.

Rnd 1: Purl.

Rnd 2: Knit.

Rnd 3: Purl. Break yarn and join color B.

Rnds 4–13: Knit. Break yarn and join color A.

Rnd 14: Knit.

Rnd 15: Purl.

Rnd 16: Knit.

Rnd 17: Purl. Break yarn and join color C.

Rnds 18–22: Knit.

Rnd 23: Purl.

BOTTOM

Pm every 8 sts.

Rnd 1: *K to 2 sts before the m, k2tog. Rep from * across the rnd. (56 sts)

Rnd 2 and all even rnds: Knit.

Rnd 3: *K to 2 sts before the m, k2tog. Rep from * across the rnd. (48 sts)

Rnd 5: *K to 2 sts before the m, k2tog. Rep from * across the rnd. (40 sts)

Rnd 7: *K to 2 sts before the m, k2tog. Rep from * across the rnd. (32 sts)

Rnd 9: *K to 2 sts before the m, k2tog. Rep from * across the rnd. (16 sts)

Rnd 11: *K2tog. Rep from * across the rnd. (8 sts)

Break yarn, leaving an 8-inch tail. Thread yarn into live sts, pull tight, and work in ends.

taxi

FINISHED MEASUREMENTS: 10-in. wide by 5-in. high
GAUGE: 5 sts = 1 inch

Rushing through the local mall near my home, I was suddenly stopped in my tracks by an adorable, funky purse in a store window. Though running late already, I dashed in to take a closer peek. It was a small purse fashioned to look like a taxi. It was silly for me to purchase it, but I did. After all these years, I still have that purse. Believe it or not, that was the inspiration for this basket. Sometimes it is nice to have something just because it makes you smile.

MATERIALS & TOOLS

- 1 skein each Brown Sheep Company, Lamb's Pride Bulky yarn (4 oz/125 yds) in the following colors:
  - 04 bulky Charcoal Heather (color A)
  - 11 bulky White Frost (color B)
  - 05 bulky Onyx (color C)
  - 155 bulky Lemon Drop (color D)
- U.S. size 6 24-in. circular needles
- Stitch markers
- #18 tapestry needle

BOTTOM AND SIDES

CO 48 sts with color A using a knitted CO. K for 48 rows. Break yarn and join color D. K across the 48 sts on the needle. Pick up and k 24 sts along the short side. Pick up and k 48 sts along the CO edge. Pick up and k 24 sts along the other short side. (144 sts) Pm. This is rnd 1 on the chart. Follow chart (below), except for the word "Taxi."

TAXI TOP

Rnd 1: After knitting the checkered pattern from the chart, break color C and knit the 3 rnds shown on the chart with color B. With color B, k 48 pm, k 24 pm, k 48 pm, k to end of round.

Rnd 2: Knit.

Rnd 3: SSK, knit to 2 sts before pm, k2tog, k24, SSK, k to 2 sts before pm, k2tog, k24. (140 sts)

Rnds 4–5: Knit.

Rnd 6: Same as rnd 3. (136 sts)

Rnd 7: Knit.

Rnd 8: Same as rnd 3. (132 sts)

Rnd 9: Knit.

Rnd 10: Same as rnd 3. (128 sts)

Rnd 11: Purl.

Rnd 12: Same as rnd 3. (124 sts)

Rnd 13: P2tog, p to 2 sts before pm, p2tog, p24, p2tog, p to 2 sts before pm, p2tog, p24 sts. (120)

Rnd 14: BO in k, decreasing same as rnd 3.

Following the chart, duplicate st the word "Taxi" on both sides of the basket.

Taxi Word Chart

The word Taxi should be centered on each long side of the basket.

= COLOR B
= COLOR C
= COLOR D

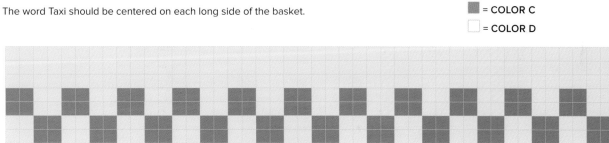

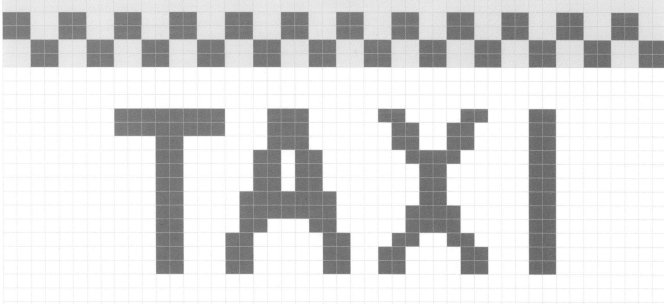

field of poppies

FINISHED MEASUREMENTS: 18-in. wide by 6-in. high
GAUGE: Not applicable due to felting

I have always loved poppies with their bright red-orange petals and black seed centers. It was easy to imagine a field of them set against an emerald field with an azure sky and puffy white clouds. My favorite story about poppies is from my husband's grandmother, who was a serf in Russia and knew the value of natural medicine. To calm down a fussy charge, she made some poppy seed tea. After sipping the hot liquid, the child not only quieted down, but fell asleep for 3 days! This basket is a tribute to her.

MATERIALS & TOOLS

- 1 skein each Cascade 220 (3½ oz/220 yds) in the following colors:
  - 8908 Anis (color A)
  - 8505 White (color B)
  - 9565 Koi (color C)
  - 2429 Irelande (color D)
  - 2445 Shire (color E)
- U.S. size 11 24-in. circular needles
- U.S. size 11 double-pointed needles
- Stitch markers
- #18 tapestry needle
- Small sewing needle
- Black quilt thread
- Tube of size 8 black beads
- Tube of 5mm black beads
- Small flower loom, such as Clover Mini Flower Loom Kit 3139
- Flower loom set, such as Clover Hana-Ami Flower Loom 3146

NOTE: 2 strands will be held tog throughout the knitted portion of the basket.

SIDES

With color A and using the circular needles, CO 144 sts. Join into round, making sure not to twist sts.

Rnd 1: *K1, bring yarn to the front and sl1, bring yarn to the back. Rep from * across the rnd.

Rnd 2: K2, *bring yarn to the front and sl1, bring yarn to the back, k1. Rep from * across the rnd.

Rep rnds 1–2 for a total of 23 rnds, ending with rnd 1. Break yarn and join 1 strand each of the colors D and E. K for 8 inches more before starting the bottom of the basket. On the last rnd pm after every 18 sts.

BOTTOM

When there are too few stitches to continue to knit in the round with the circular needles, switch to dpn.

Rnd 1: *K to 2 sts before pm, k2tog. Rep from * across the rnd. (136 sts)

Rnd 2: Knit.

Rnd 3: *K to 2 sts before pm, k2tog. Rep from * across the rnd. (128 sts)

Rnd 4: Knit.

Rnd 5: *K to 2 sts before pm, k2tog. Rep from * across the rnd. (120 sts)

Rnd 6: Knit.

Rnd 7: *K to 2 sts before pm, k2tog. Rep from * across the rnd. (112 sts)

Rnd 8: Knit.

Rnd 9: *K to 2 sts before pm, k2tog. Rep from * across the rnd. (104 sts)

Rnd 10: Knit.

Rnd 11: *K to 2 sts before pm, k2tog. Rep from * across the rnd. (96 sts)

Rnd 12: Knit.

Rnd 13: *K to 2 sts before pm, k2tog. Rep from * across the rnd. (88 sts)

Rnd 14: Knit.

Rnd 15: *K to 2 sts before pm, k2tog. Rep from * across the rnd. (80 sts)

Rnd 16: Knit.

Rnd 17: *K to 2 sts before pm, k2tog. Rep from * across the rnd. (72 sts)

Rnd 18: Knit.

Rnd 19: *K to 2 sts before pm, k2tog. Rep from * across the rnd. (64 sts)

Rnd 20: Knit.

Rnd 21: *K to 2 sts before pm, k2tog. Rep from * across the rnd. (56 sts)

Rnd 22: Knit.

Rnd 23: *K to 2 sts before pm, k2tog. Rep from * across the rnd. (48 sts)

Rnd 24: Knit.

Rnd 25: *K to 2 sts before pm, k2tog. Rep from * across the rnd. (40 sts)

Rnd 26: Knit.

Rnd 27: *K to 2 sts before pm, k2tog. Rep from * across the rnd. (32 sts)

Rnd 28: Knit.

Rnd 29: *K to 2 sts before pm, k2tog. Rep from * across the rnd. (24 sts)

Rnd 30: Knit.

Rnd 31: *K to 2 sts before pm, k2tog. Rep from * across the rnd. (16 sts)

Rnd 32: Knit.

Rnd 33: *K2tog. Rep from * across the rnd. (8 sts)

Break yarn, leaving an 8-inch tail. Weave yarn into live sts and pull tight to close. Work in ends.

CLOUDS

Using 1 strand of color B, follow the chart (at right) to cross-stitch clouds. There will be a total of 4 reps of the cloud chart. Make sure to cross-stitch somewhat loosely so the clouds will felt better.

FELTING

Wet-felt the basket until it matches finished measurement sizes or to desired size (page 16).

Cloud Chart

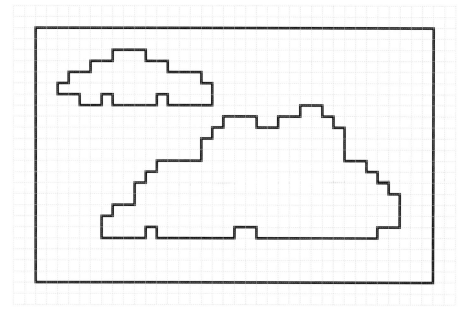

Repeat a total of 4 times.

POPPIES

Make the desired number of poppies using both the circular small flower loom, such as the Mini Flower Loom, and the smallest circle in the flower loom set, such as the Hana-Ami loom. Use 1 yard of color C for the small poppies and 1⅔ yards for the large poppies. Insert tail into groove on the edge of the looms. Wind yarn as per instructions that come with the looms. Thread tapestry needle with yarn and insert needle to the WS between loops near the beginning. Come up between loops across from the beginning. Pull slightly to center loops that became slightly off-center when winding the yarn around the pegs. Start weaving over and under, making sure to include the tail as a strand in the weaving. This is important, because an odd number of strands is needed for the weaving. Continue weaving until there is about 4 inches of yarn left. Take off loom and work ends into the back of the poppy.

Sew 3 smaller beads in the center of each smaller poppy and 3 of the larger beads in the center of each larger poppy using black quilting thread. With thread, sew poppies as desired to the green field portion of the basket.

aran basket

FINISHED MEASUREMENTS: 6½-in. wide by 4-in. high
GAUGE: 5 sts = 1 inch

Born in the rugged islands off the western coast of Ireland, most inhabitants were either fishermen or farmers. The Aran sweater was born out of necessity to keep the fishermen both dry and warm against northern Atlantic gales. They were more than just a practical garment, however, with the maker knitting ancient patterns reflective of the Celtic culture. Both patterns and sweaters were passed down for generations. These amazing pieces of knitting boasted around 100,000 stitches in a single sweater. Our basket does not have nearly that amount of stitches, but it does reflect a little of the beauty of the Aran fisherman's sweater.

MATERIALS & TOOLS

- 2 skeins Brown Sheep Company, Lamb's Pride Worsted yarn (4 oz/190 yds) in M01 Sandy Heather
- U.S. size 6 20-in. circular needles
- U.S. size 6 double-pointed needles
- Cable needle
- Stitch markers
- Yarn needle

NOTE: Hold 2 strands tog throughout the basket.

SIDES

Using the circular needles, CO 96 sts.

Rnd 1: *K2, p2. Rep from * across the rnd. Rep row 1 until basket measures 3 inches.

CABLE SECTION

Rnd 1: Knit.

Rnd 2: Same as rnd 1.

Rnd 3: *K2, place 2 sts onto cable needle and hold in back, k next 2 sts, k 2 sts from cable needle. Rep from * across the rnd.

Rnd 4: Same as rnd 1.

Rnd 5: Same as rnd 1.

Rnd 6: Same as rnd 1.

Rnd 7: *Place 2 sts onto cable needle and hold in front, k next 2 sts, k 2 sts from cable needle, k2. Rep from * across the rnd.

Rnd 8: Same as rnd 1.

Rep rnds 1–8 once more.

BOTTOM

Switch to dpn; pm every 12 sts.

Rnd 1: *K to 2 sts before the m, k2tog. Rep from * across the rnd. (88 sts)

Rnd 2 and all even rnds: Knit.

Rnd 3: Same as rnd 1. (80 sts)

Rnd 5: Same as rnd 1. (72 sts)

Rnd 7: Same as rnd 1. (64 sts)

Rnd 9: Same as rnd 1. (56 sts)

Rnd 11: Same as rnd 1. (48 sts)

Rnd 13: Same as rnd 1. (40 sts)

Rnd 15: Same as rnd 1. (32 sts)

Rnd 17: Same as rnd 1. (24 sts)

Rnd 19: Same as rnd 1. (16 sts)

Rnd 21: Same as rnd 1. (8 sts)

Break yarn and thread through live sts and pull tight. Work in ends. Steam basket to shape. Turn half of the ribbing to the outside of the basket.

mcbasket

FINISHED MEASUREMENTS: 9-in. wide by 5-in. high
GAUGE: 3 sts in garter stitch = 1 inch

It all depends on which side of the pond you are whether you use the word "plaid" or "tartan." In America, plaid, a Gaelic word for "blanket," is the preferred term, but in Scotland, it is tartan. Whichever term you use, they both refer to the beautiful woven wools used for kilts and clan identification.

Our hope is that knitting this basket will transport you to the highlands of Scotland. To better set the mood, why not watch *Brigadoon, Hamish Macbeth, Braveheart, Rob Roy* or *Outlander* while knitting. You can almost smell the heather.

MATERIALS & TOOLS

- 1 skein Red Heart Super Saver yarn (7 oz/364 yds) in 319 Cherry Red
- ⅛ yds (60-in. wide) each of 6 different wool plaid fabrics
- U.S. size 9 double-pointed needles
- U.S. size 9 24-in. circular needles
- U.S. size 10 straight or circular needles
- Stitch marker
- #13 tapestry needle

NOTE: Hold 2 strands tog throughout the basket.

PREPARING THE WOOL FABRIC

Cut wool fabric into ½ by 3-inch pieces. Toss pieces like a salad to mix up the different plaids.

BOTTOM

CO 8 sts onto dpn, distributing them evenly over 4 needles.

Rnd 1: Join into round, making sure not to twist the sts. Knit.

Rnd 2: KFB each st. (16 sts)

Rnds 3–5: Knit.

Rnd 6: Same as rnd 2. (32 sts)

Rnds 7–10: Knit.

Rnd 11: Same as rnd 2. (64 sts)

Rnds 12–16: Knit.

Rnd 17: *K1, kfb. Rep from * across the rnd. (96 sts)

Rnds 18–23: Knit.

Rnd 24: Purl. At this point, turn the basket inside out. The basket will be worked from now on with the RS of the basket facing in toward the center with the WS on the outside. When completed, turn the basket RS out.

Rnd 25: Sl the first st pwise; p the rest of the rnd, breaking yarn at some point during this rnd to string on wool strips. Using the tapestry needle, thread on 96 wool strips in the center of the strip. You may add more if you don't mind continuously sliding the wool strips down while knitting the basket. You will need 48 strips per rnd where strips appear.

SIDES

Rnd 1: Using U.S. size 9 circular needles, *K1, slide a wool strip up next to the right needle, k1. Rep from * across the rnd. Strip will automatically go to the RS, which is on the inside right now.

Rnd 2: Purl.

Rnd 3: *Slide a wool strip up next to the right needle, k1, k1. Rep from * across the rnd.

Rnd 4: Purl.

Rep rnds 1–4 until basket measures about 4½ inches.

K 1 rnd.

P 1 rnd.

BO using the U.S. size 10 needle in your right hand (keep a size 9 in your left).

origami travel basket

FINISHED MEASUREMENTS: 6-in. wide by 4-in. high
GAUGE: 5 sts in garter stitch = 1 inch

This basket is a combination of a few inspirations. When I was a child, my grandparents gave me a book about the Japanese art of origami. I couldn't wait to start folding my own paper creations. This was the beginning of a life-long love of origami. So where does the "travel" part come from? There have been times when I would have loved to have a basket on some of my travels. When throwing it into your suitcase, just unsnap it to lay flat. When you need it to be a basket, just snap up the sides—practical and elegant.

MATERIALS & TOOLS

- 2 skeins Cascade 220 yarn (3½ oz/220 yds) in 8872 Iridescence
- U.S. size 5 needles
- U.S. size 6 needles
- Stitch marker
- Matching thread
- Sewing needle
- 4 snaps, size 10

PLACEMENT ILLUSTRATION

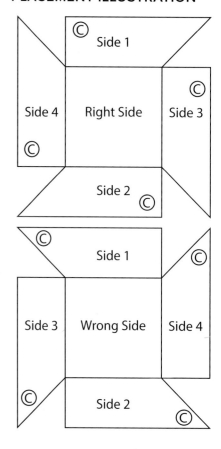

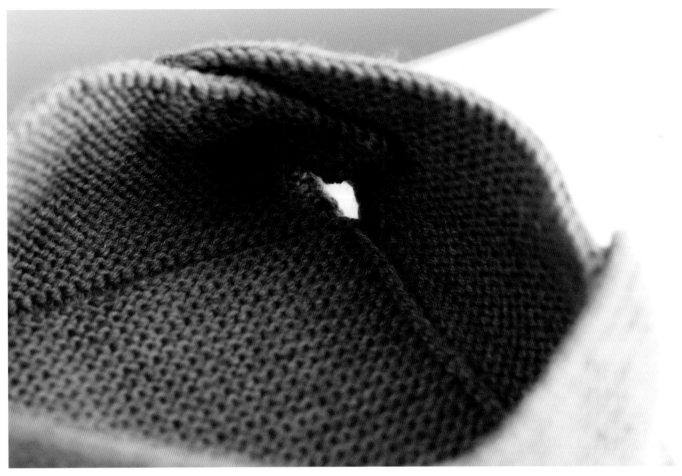

SIDE 1

CO 45 sts using the smaller needles.

Row 1: Sl1, k to the end. (RS)

Rows 2–4: Same as row 1.

Row 5: Sl1, k2tog, k to the end of the row. (44 sts)

Row 6: Sl1, k to the end.

Rep rows 5–6 until the piece has 30 sts rem.

P 1 row, slipping the first st. (RS)

K 1 row, slipping the first st. (WS)

BOTTOM

Sl1, k to the end. Rep this row for a total of 60 rows, ending with a WS row completed.

P 1 row, slipping the first st.

K 1 row, slipping the first st.

SIDE 2

Row 1: Sl1, k to last 2 sts, kfb, k1. (31 sts) (RS)

Row 2: Sl1, k across the row.

Rep rows 1–2 until the piece has 45 sts rem.

K 4 rows even, slipping the first st.

BO loosely, using a U.S. size 6 needle.

SIDE 3

Place piece on a flat surface with the RS facing up. Turn piece 90° to the right. Pick up and k 30 sts along the bottom edge, working from left to right to pick up sts. If needed, use a crochet hook to pick up sts. Follow directions for side 2.

SIDE 4

Place piece on a flat surface with RS facing up and the side 3 closest to you. Turn piece 180°. Pick up sts as for side 3. Follow directions for side 2.

FINISHING

Using matching sewing thread, sew the male part of the snap to each triangular WS corner. Sew the female part of the snap to each RS 2 inches in from the square corner right below the top edge.

Snap tog as desired.

berry basket

FINISHED MEASUREMENTS: 4½-in. wide by 3-in. high

GAUGE: 5 sts = 1 inch

Two of my favorite fruit families are citrus and berries. If I had to choose between the two, it certainly would be a hard choice, but I think the berries would win out. Blueberries, strawberries, raspberries, and blackberries top that list. I just can't wait until the summertime, when luscious berries are abundant. This basket's texture mimics the raspberry. Although it would not be good for gathering freshly picked berries, it can handily hold a number of other things. I suggest a bowl of yummy berries as a treat after completing this basket—you deserve it.

MATERIALS & TOOLS

- 1 skein each Cascade 220 yarn (3½ oz/220 yds) in the following colors:
  - 2449 Peony Pink (color A)
  - 2420 Heather (color B)
- U.S. size 5 double-pointed needles
- U.S. size 5 16- or 20-in. circular needles
- Yarn needles

NOTE: Hold 2 strands tog throughout. After knitting the bottom of the basket, the berry st will be worked on the WS. When basket is completed, turn basket RS out.

Knitted by Megan Senini.

BOTTOM

With color B, CO 8 sts onto dpn, distributing evenly over 4 needles.

Rnd 1: Join into round, making sure not to twist sts. Knit.

Rnd 2: KFB each st. (16 sts)

Rnds 3–5: Knit.

Rnd 6: Same as rnd 2. (32 sts)

Rnds 7–10: Knit.

Rnd 11: Same as rnd 2. (64 sts)

Rnds 12–16: Knit. Break color B and join color A. Reverse direction of knitting so that the outside of the basket is facing in toward the center. The inside of the basket bottom should be facing down as you are knitting with the RS facing up.

SIDES

Rnd 1: Knit.

Rnd 2: *(K1, p1, k1) into next st, p3tog. Rep from * across the rnd.

Rnd 3: Knit.

Rnd 4: *P3tog, (k1, p1, k1) into next st. Rep from * across the rnd.

Rep these 4 rows 5 times. Break yarn and join color B. Rep rows 1–3 1 time with row 4 of the last rep as the BO row. Weave in ends. Turn basket right side out.

nesting modular baskets

FINISHED MEASUREMENTS: From large to small: 10-in. wide by 10-in. high; 5-in. wide by 5-in. high; 2½-in. wide by 2½-in. high

GAUGE: Not applicable

I know it isn't necessary, but I take great pains with my knitting to avoid assembling and finishing. The discovery of modular knitting was a pivotal moment for me. Throw into the mix a love of matryoshka dolls—those nesting painted dolls from Russia—and a touch of geometry, and you end up with these baskets. If you are like me, you'll love knitting up these nesting baskets, as there is little more to do than work in your ends when completed!

MATERIALS & TOOLS

- Cascade 220 yarn (3½ oz/220 yds) in the following colors:
  - 2 skeins 7811 Purple Jewel Heather (color A)
  - 1 skein 7803 Magenta (color B)
  - 1 skein 9488 Christmas Red Heather (color C)
  - 1 skein 2429 Irelande (color D)
  - 1 skein 9444 Tangerine Heather (color E)
  - 1 skein 4010 Straw (color F)
  - 1 skein 9449 Midnight Heather (color G)
- U.S. size 10 24-in. circular needles
- U.S. size 10 36-in. circular needles
- Yarn needle
- Smooth contrasting scrap yarn
- Size I crochet hook
- Stitch marker

Knitted by Priscilla Pietz.

Rep row 2 until 24 (48, 96) rows have been completed, including row 1. Do not BO. Break yarn. With color B, k across live sts on the needle. CO 12 (24, 48) sts. Follow directions for the large square to create square 1 (page 111). Side 1 is a single large square—square 1 on the chart. Break yarn.

SIDE 2

Side 2 is a grid of 4 small squares. Start by creating square 2. Using color E and working to the right of the first large square 1 and with the RS (outside) of the basket facing, pick up and k 6 (12, 24) sts starting in the middle of side 2 and working to the left. Pick up and k 6 (12, 24) sts along the lower half of large square 1. Follow directions for small square (page 111). When 1 st remains, do not BO. Break yarn.

Create square 3. Using color D, pick up and k 5 (11, 23) sts more along the top of the small square just completed. Pick up and k 6 (12, 24) sts along the RH edge of large square 1. Follow directions for small square (page 111). Break yarn.

Create square 4. Using color G and working from the right corner of side 2 toward the center, pick up and k 6 (12, 24) sts. Pick up and k 6 (12, 24) sts along the RS of small square 4. When 1 st remains, do not BO. Break yarn.

Create square 5. Using color F, pick up and k 5 (11, 23) sts more along the top of the small square just completed. Pick up and k 6 (12, 24) sts along the RH edge of small square 3. Break yarn.

NOTE: Since this is knit as a modular piece, there will be no sewing when completed. Use the chart (below) for both color placement and order of knitting. All baskets start with the bottom knitted first. The 24-inch circular needles will be used throughout, except for the I-cord BO on the large basket. Directions for the small basket are outside the parenthesis and directions for the medium and large are inside. A knitted CO will be used throughout.

BOTTOM AND SIDE 1

Using scrap yarn and a crochet hook, chain 18 (30, 54) sts. Using color A, pick up 12 (24, 48) sts through the bottom loops of the chain. Make sure to pick up on the bottom of the chain so this crocheted provisional CO can be easily removed later. The reason for chaining more chains than stitches being picked up is because it is easier to pick up those stitches with chain stitches on either side.

Row 1: K to last st, p. (WS)

Row 2: Sl1 kwise, k to last st, p. (RS)

PLACEMENT ILLUSTRATION

Large Square 1 Color B	Small Square 3 Color D	Small Square 5 Color F	Large Square 6 Color C	Rectangle 8 Color D	Large Square 1
	Small Square 2 Color E	Small Square 4 Color G		Rectangle 7 Color F	
Side 1	Side 2		Side 3	Side 4	

SIDE 3

Turn basket to side 3, which is made of one large square—square 6. Using color C and working from right to left, pick up and k 12 (24, 48) sts. Pick up and k 12 (24, 48) sts along the RS of small squares 4 and 5. Follow directions for large square (page 111). Break yarn.

SIDE 4

Turn basket to side 4, which is composed of 2 rectangles. Create rectangle 7. Using color F, pick up and k 6 (12, 24) sts along the left edge of large square 1. This will join the basket in the rnd. Pick up and k 12 (24, 48) sts along the bottom edge of the basket, and pick up and k 6 (12, 24) sts along the lower half of large square 6. Follow directions for the rectangle (page 111). Break yarn.

Create rectangle 8. Using color D, pick up and k 6 (12, 24) sts along the upper half of large square 1. Pick up and k 12 (24, 48) sts along the top edge of rectangle 7. Pick up and k 6 (12, 24) sts along the upper half of large square 6. Follow directions for the rectangle (page 111). Break yarn.

Using color A and starting in the middle of large square 1, pick up and k 6 (12, 24) to the corner. Pick up and k 12 (24, 48) sts along each of side 2, 3, and 4. Pick up and k 6 (12, 24) sts along the right half of side 1. You should have 48 (96, 192) sts. Join by CO 3 sts. BO sts using I-cord BO (page 15).

Wet-felt in washing machine (page 16). Stuff with plastic bags to hold shape while drying.

LARGE SQUARE

Using a knitted CO, CO 24 (48, 96) sts; pm between the middle 2 sts.

Row 1 (WS): K to last st, p.

Row 2 (RS): Sl1 kwise, k to 2 sts before m, ssk, slip m, k2tog, k to last st, p.

Row 3: Sl1 kwise, k to last st, p.

Rep rows 2–3 until 4 sts remain. SSK, k2tog.

Next row, k2tog. Break yarn and pull through.

SMALL SQUARE

Using a knitted CO, CO 12 (24, 48) sts; pm between the middle 2 sts.

Row 1 (WS): K to last st, p.

Row 2 (RS): Sl1 kwise, k to 2 sts before m, ssk, slip m, k2tog, k to last st, p.

Row 3: Sl1 kwise, k to last st, p.

Rep rows 2–3 until 4 sts remain. SSK, k2tog.

Next row, k2tog. Break yarn and pull through.

RECTANGLE

Using a knitted CO, CO 24 (48, 96) sts; pm between the 6th and 7th (12th and 13th, 24th and 25th) sts and the 18th and 19th (36th and 37th, 72nd and 73rd) sts.

Row 1 (WS): K to last st, p.

Row 2 (RS): Sl1 kwise, k to 2 sts before first m, ssk, slip m, k2tog, k to 2 sts before next m, ssk, slip m, k2tog, k to last st, p.

Row 3: Sl1 kwise, k to last st, p.

Rep rows 2–3 until 4 sts remain after last dec. Do not knit back on these sts. Bind them off by sl1, k1, psso. Rep once more. K2tog. Break yarn.

seurat reimagined

FINISHED MEASUREMENTS: 8-in. wide by 5-in. high
GAUGE: 3 sts = 1 inch

Georges Seurat, a post-Impressionist painter, is best known for pointillism, in which he painted his pictures with very tiny dots. No small feat, considering the size of some of his paintings. His paintings practically shimmer from the effect of placing dots of complementary colors next to each other. This basket is a visual pun with small "dots" of color created by the scrappy yarn next to other colors. Added to this are the bobbles, symbolizing larger dots. Not to worry when creating this basket—it knits up quickly, unlike some of Seurat's most famous paintings.

MATERIALS & TOOLS

- 1 skein Red Heart Super Saver yarn (7 oz/364 yds) in 312 Black
- 1 skein scrappy yarn approx 300 yds (see instructions)
- #18 tapestry needle
- U.S. size 9 24-in. circular needles
- U.S. size 9 double-pointed needles
- Stitch markers
- Yarn needle

NOTE: Hold 2 strands tog throughout the basket.

MAKING SCRAPPY YARN

To make scrappy yarn, use a Russian join to join scraps of yarn. Thread 1 piece of yarn onto the tapestry needle, leaving as short a tail as possible. Lay a 2nd piece of yarn on top of the first piece and under the needle. Sew back into the yarn for about 2 inches and pull yarn through. Pull tight. Thread the 2nd piece of yarn, leaving as short a tail as possible. Sew back into the yarn for about 2 inches and pull yarn through. Pull tight. You have completed 1 join. Continue to join pieces of yarn until you have a large skein of yarn about 300 yards. If you run out of scrappy yarn before completing your basket, just add more yarn to the ends.

SIDES

With the black yarn and circular needles, CO 88 sts and join into round, making sure not to twist.

K 10 rows.

Next row, *k11, M1. Rep from * across the row. (96 sts)

K 1 more row of black. Break yarn and join scrappy yarn.

Rows 1–2: Knit.

Row 3: *K5, make bobble (at right). Rep from * across the rnd.

Rows 4–5: Knit.

Row 6: K2, *make bobble, k5. Rep from * until 4 sts remain. Make bobble, k3.

Rows 7–8: Knit.

Rep rows 3–8 2 times more for a total of 6 rows of bobbles. Pm every 12 sts. Switch to dpn as needed.

BASKET BOTTOM

Rnd 1: *K to 2 sts before the m, k2tog. Rep from * across the rnd. (88 sts)

Rnd 2 and all even rnds: Knit.

Rnd 3: Same as rnd 1. (80 sts)

Rnd 5: Same as rnd 1. (72 sts)

Rnd 7: Same as rnd 1. (64 sts)

Rnd 9: Same as rnd 1. (56 sts)

Rnd 11: Same as rnd 1. (48 sts)

Rnd 13: Same as rnd 1. (40 sts)

Rnd 15: Same as rnd 1. (32 sts)

Rnd 17: Same as rnd 1. (24 sts)

Rnd 19: Same as rnd 1. (16 sts)

Rnd 21: *K2tog. Rep from * across the rnd. (8 sts) Break yarn leaving an 8-inch tail. Thread tail through live sts. Pull tight and work in ends.

BOBBLE

To make a bobble, k into the front, back, and front of the next st. Turn work and p back. Turn work. Slip the first 2 sts pwise, k1, and pass slipped sts over the k st.

pumpkin baskets

FINISHED MEASUREMENTS: Large: 8 x 4-in. basket, 14-in. vine, 6 x 7-in. leaf; Small: 6 x 3-in. basket, 10-in. vine, 4 x 4¼-in. leaf

GAUGE: Not applicable

Nothing says autumn like pumpkins. In farmers' fields each fall, against a clear blue sky and crisp air, thousands of bright orange pumpkins lay on the ground waiting to be carried to someone's home. Part of the squash family, the pumpkin is both decorative and delicious to eat in the form of pumpkin pie and toasted seeds. As fall turns to winter, the pumpkins shrivel and are thrown out, but knitting your own pumpkin basket keeps the spirit of autumn alive all year round.

MATERIALS & TOOLS

- Cascade 220 yarn (3½ oz/220 yds) in the following colors:
  - 2 skeins 9444 Tangerine Heather (color A)
  - 1 skein 2435 Japanese Maple (color B)
  - 1 skein 2429 Irelande (color C)
  - 1 skein 2445 Shire (color D)

For smaller basket:

- U.S. size 10 16-in. circular needles
- U.S. size 10 24-in. circular needles
- U.S. size 10 double-pointed needles

For larger basket:

- U.S. size 13 16-in. circular needles
- U.S. size 13 24-in. circular needles
- U.S. size 13 double-pointed needles

- Stitch markers
- 1 yard smooth waste yarn
- Size I crochet hook
- Yarn needle

NOTE: For small basket, use 1 strand throughout, using color C for the vine. Use 2 strands for larger basket, holding 1 each of colors C and D tog for the vine. Use the circular needles or dpn as needed.

PUMPKIN

Using scrap yarn and crochet hook, chain 60. Using color A, pick up 56 sts through the bottom loops of the chain. Make sure to pick up on the bottom of the chain to remove more easily later.

Rnd 1: Join into round and k with circular needles.

Rnd 2: KFB, k27, kfb, k to end of rnd. (58 sts)

Rnd 3: *K2, kfb. Rep from * 18 times more, k1. (77 sts)

Rnd 4: *K24, kfb. Rep from * 2 more times, k2. (80 sts)

Rnds 5–16: *P1, k7. Rep from * to the end of the rnd.

Rnd 17: *P1, k5, k2tog. Rep from * to end of the rnd. (70 sts)

Rnds 18–21: Knit.

Rnd 22: *P1, k4, k2tog. Rep from * to the end of the rnd. (60 sts)

Rnds 23–26: Switch to dpn. Knit.

Rnd 27: *P1, k3, k2tog. Rep from * to the end of the rnd. (50 sts)

Rnds 28–31: Knit.

Rnd 32: *P1, k2, k2tog. Rep from * to the end of the rnd. (40 sts)

Rnd 33: Knit.

Rnd 34: *K3, k2tog. Rep from * to the end of the rnd. (32 sts)

Rnd 35: Knit.

Rnd 36: *K2, k2tog. Rep from * to the end of the rnd. (24 sts)

Rnd 37: Knit.

Rnd 38: *K1, k2tog. Rep from * to the end of the rnd. (16 sts)

Rnd 39: *K2tog. Rep from * to the end of the rnd. (8 sts)

Cut the yarn tail and use a yarn needle to thread through all 8 sts and pull tight to close, weaving in ends securely.

VINE

Remove waste yarn at the top of the basket. Using appropriately sized dpn, pick up and k 56 sts using color C. Using a knitted CO, CO 3 sts. BO 28 sts using an I-cord BO. Switch to knitting an I-cord for 4 inches. This will create a loop. Resume I-cord BO on the 29th st to the end of the rnd. Work I-cord for 16(20) inches. On the last row of the I-cord, k1, M1, k1, M1, k1. (5 sts)

P 1 row.

LEAF

Row 1: KFB twice, k1, kfb twice. (9 sts)

Row 2: Purl.

Row 3: KFB 4 times, k1, kfb 4 times. (17 sts)

Row 4: Purl.

Row 5: KFB 8 times, k1, kfb 8 times. (33 sts)

Row 6: Purl.

Row 7: Knit.

Row 8: Purl.

Row 9: BO 3 sts at the beginning of the row. K to the end. (30 sts)

Row 10: BO 3 sts at the beginning of the row. P to the end. (27 sts)

Row 11: Knit.

Row 12: Purl.

Row 13: Knit.

Row 14: Purl.

Row 15: BO 3 sts at the beginning of the row. K to the end. (24 sts)

Row 16: BO 3 sts at the beginning of the row. P to the end. (21 sts)

Row 17: Knit.

Row 18: Purl.

Row 19: Knit.

Row 20: Purl.

Row 21: BO 3 sts at the beginning of the row. K to the end. (18 sts)

Row 22: BO 3 sts at the beginning of the row. K to the end. (15 sts)

Row 23: Knit.

Row 24: Purl.

Row 25: Knit.

Row 26: Purl.

Row 27: BO 3 sts at the beginning of the row. K to the end. (12 sts)

Row 28: BO 3 sts at the beginning of the row. P to the end. (9 sts)

Row 29: Knit.

Row 30: Purl.

Row 31: BO 3 sts at the beginning of the row. K to the end. (6 sts)

Row 32: BO 3 sts at the beginning of the row. P to the end. (3 sts)

Row 33: Knit.

Row 34: Purl.

Row 35: Sl1, k2tog, psso. Break yarn and pull through last st.

FINISHING

Before felting, work in all ends. Using color B, do a running st in the p "troughs," carrying the yarn loosely from one trough to the next. Thread leaf through the short loop of the basket. Wet-felt (page 16). Shape and stuff with plastic bags to dry.

tiffany lamp baskets

FINISHED MEASUREMENTS: From large to small: 12-in. wide by 7½-in. high; 9-in. wide by 5½-in. high; 6½-in. wide by 4-in. high

GAUGE: 3½ sts in stockinette = 1 inch

What a find to discover the Morse Museum in Winter Park, Florida. This sometimes-overlooked treasure in suburban Orlando is full of Louis Comfort Tiffany treasures, including his famous leaded stained glass lamps. These brightly colored lamps were the inspiration for these baskets. To create the effect of stained glass, each tier of the basket is knit with 2 variegated yarns framed by black to mimic the leading.

MATERIALS & TOOLS

- Red Heart Super Saver yarn (7 oz/364 yds) in the following colors:
  - 2 skeins 312 Black (color A)
  - 1 skein 2187 Razzle (color B)*
  - 1 skein 3952 Icelandic (color C)
  - 1 skein 3953 Butterfly (color D)
  - 1 skein 301 Mirage (color E)
  - 1 skein 994 Banana Berry Print (color F)
  - 1 skein 315 Artist Print (color G)
  - 1 skein 996 Sedona (color H)*
  - 1 skein 318 Watercolor (color I)
- U.S. size 9 double-pointed needles
- U.S. size 9 16-in. circular needles
- U.S. size 9 24-in. circular needles
- U.S. size 7 24-in. circular needles
- Yarn needle

*These colors have been discontinued. Please select a multi-colored yarn you prefer instead.

NOTE: Hold 2 strands tog throughout the basket.

BOTTOM

As you progress, switch to the U.S. size 9 16- and 24-inch circular needles as required.

With color A, CO 8 sts onto dpn, distributing evenly over 4 needles.

Rnd 1: Join into round, making sure not to twist the sts. K.

Rnd 2: KFB each st. (16 st)

Rnds 3–5: Knit.

Rnd 6: Same as rnd 2. (32 sts)

Rnds 7–10: Knit.

Rnd 11: Same as rnd 2. (64 sts)

Rnds 12–16: Knit.

End small basket bottom here and go to rnd 30.

Rnd 17: *K1, kfb. Rep from * across the rnd. (96 sts)

Rnds 18–23: Knit.

End medium basket bottom here and go to rnd 30.

Rnd 24: *K2, kfb. Rep from * across the rnd. (128 sts)

Rnds 25–29: Knit.

Rnd 30: Purl.

SIDES

Rnds 31–33: Knit. Break color A and join colors B and C.

Rnds 34–39: Knit. Break colors B and C and join color A.

Rnd 40: K3, *drop the next st to be knitted that is on the left needle down 6 rows to the black. Insert right needle into the loop of black from front to back and under the horizontal bars of yarn created by the dropped st. YO; pull under the horizontal rows and back through the loop to the front of the work. Place this last st made onto the left needle and k1. K7. Rep from * 14 times more. Follow directions for dropping a st once more. K4.

Rnds 41–42: Knit. Break color A and join colors D and E.

End small basket sides and go to rnd 67 to finish.

Rnds 43–51: Rep rnds 34–42. Break yarn after completing rnd 51 and join colors F and G.

End medium basket sides and go to rnd 67 to finish.

Rnds 52–60: Rep rnds 34–42. Break yarn after completing rnd 60 and join colors H and I.

Rnds 61–66: Knit. Break yarn after completing rnd 66 and join color A.

Rnd 67: Same as rnd 40. Switch to U.S. size 7 needles for the last rnds.

Rnd 68: Purl.

Rnd 69: Knit.

Rnd 70: Purl.

BO loosely. Work in ends.

resources

ABBREVIATIONS

*Repeat instructions following the asterisk[s] as directed

BO	bind off		pwise	purlwise
CO	cast on		rem	remain/remaining
cont	continue		rep	repeat(s)
dec	decrease(s)		RH	right hand
dpn	double-pointed needle(s)		rnd(s)	round(s)
inc	increase(s)		RS	right side
k	knit		sl	slip
k2tog	knit 2 stitches together		sl st	slip stitch(es)
kfb	knit in front and back		ssk	slip, slip, knit these 2 stiches together—a decrease
kwise	knitwise			
LH	left hand		st(s)	stitch(es)
m M1	marker make one stitch		tog	together
mm	millimeter(s)		WS	wrong side
oz	ounce(s)		wyib	with yarn in back
p	purl		wyif	with yarn in front
pm	place marker		yd(s)	yard(s)
p2tog	purl 2 stitches together		yo	yarn over
psso	pass slipped stitch over			

KNITTING NEEDLE SIZES

Millimeter	U.S. Size*
2.25 mm	B-1
2.75 mm	C-2
3.25 mm	D-3
3.5 mm	E-4
3.75 mm	F-5
4 mm	G-6
4.5 mm	7
5 mm	H-8
5.5 mm	I-9
6 mm	J-10
6.5 mm	K-10½
8 mm	L-11
9 mm	M/N-13

*Number may vary. Rely on the mm sizing.

YARN WEIGHT CHART

Yarn Weight Symbol & Category Names	0 LACE	1 SUPER FINE	2 FINE	3 LIGHT	4 MEDIUM	5 BULKY	6 SUPER BULKY	7 JUMBO
Types of Yarns in Category	Fingering, 10 count crochet thread	Sock, Fingering, Baby	Sport, Baby	DK, Light Worsted	Worsted, Afghan, Aran	Chunky, Craft, Rug	Bulky, Roving	Jumbo, Roving

Source: Craft Yarn Council's www.YarnStandards.com

METRIC CONVERSIONS

In this book, we've used inches, yards, and ounces, showing anything less than one as a fraction. If you want to convert those to metric measurements, please use the following formulas:

FRACTIONS TO DECIMALS

⅛ = .125
¼ = .25
½ = .5
⅝ = .625
¾ = .75

IMPERIAL TO METRIC CONVERSION

LENGTH

Multiply inches by 25.4 to get millimeters
Multiply inches by 2.54 to get centimeters
Multiply yards by .9144 to get meters

For example, if you wanted to convert 1⅛ inches to millimeters:
- 1.125 in. x 25.4 mm = 28.575 mm

And to convert 2½ yards to meters:
- 2.5 yd. x .9144 m = 2.286 m

WEIGHT

Multiply ounces by 28.35 to get grams

For example, if you wanted to convert 5 ounces to grams:
- 5 oz. x 28.35 g = 141.75 g

SUPPLIERS

Bee Line Art Tools
866-218-1590
www.beelinearttools.com

Berroco, Inc.
401-769-1212
www.berroco.com

Brown Sheep Company, Inc.
www.brownsheep.com

Cascade Yarn
www.cascadeyarns.com

Clover Needlecraft, Inc.
800-233-1703
www.clover-usa.com

Coats and Clark
www.makeitcoats.com

Denise Interchangeable Knitting and Crochet
www.knitdenise.com

Dewberry Ridge
636-583-8112
www.dewberryridge.com

Dorr Mill Store
800-846-3677
www.dorrmillstore.com

Jelly Yarn
215-953-1415
www.jellyyarns.com

Lacis
510-843-7178
www.lacis.com

Let Nola Do It, LLC
www.nolahooks.com

Lion Brand Yarns
www.lionbrand.com

PattieWack Designs
www.pattiewack.com

Skif International
314-773-4401
www.skifo.com

Wool Novelty Company
800-831-1135
www.weavingloops.com

While specified brands of yarn were used in the making of the baskets in this book, feel free to use your favorite brand of yarn. (Available online and through your local yarn shop.)

about the authors

Nola Heidbreder has been teaching fiber art and handwork both across the country and from her studio in St. Louis, Missouri, for more than 20 years. She has written articles and projects for *Mary Englebreit's Home Companion* and *Rug Hooking* magazine, contributed to the popular book *Finishing Hooked Rugs*, and has appeared on local and national television. To learn more about Nola and her work, visit nolahooks.com.

Linda Pietz learned to knit at the age of four and has spent more than 40 years passing along her love of knitting and other crafts through classes and workshops. She designs patterns for Bucilla, Dimensions, Cat's Cradle, and other companies, and has been featured in several books, including *Gourds + Fiber*. Linda has written articles for *Rug Hooking* magazine and other national magazines. She currently lives in northern California.

In addition to co-authoring Crochet Baskets *and* Knitted Baskets *for Spring House Press, Nola and Linda have collaborated to create* Knitting Rugs: 39 Traditional, Contemporary, Innovative Designs *and* Crocheting Rugs: 40 Traditional, Contemporary, Innovative Designs. *In 2013, they completed "Hooking the Presidents," an amazing collection of rug-hooked portraits of all 44 Presidents that toured the country and received media attention both locally and nationally.*

index

MORE GREAT BOOKS *from*
SPRING HOUSE PRESS

Christmas Ornaments to Crochet
978-1940611-48-8
$22.95 | 136 Pages

Construction Vehicles to Crochet
978-1-940611-57-0
$22.95 | 128 Pages

Emoji Crochet
978-1-940611-72-3
$19.95 | 128 Pages

Crochet Baskets
978-1940611-61-7
$22.95 | 128 Pages

Zippy Loom Creations
978-1-940611-79-2
$16.99 | 88 Pages

Afghan Loom Projects
978-1-940611-78-5
$14.99 | 72 pages

SPRING HOUSE PRESS

Look for these Spring House Press titles at your favorite bookstore, specialty retailer,
or visit *www.springhousepress.com*.

For more information about Spring House Press, email us at *info@springhousepress.com*.